artists' houses

artists'
houses

Gérard-Georges Lemaire

PHOTOGRAPHS BY Jean-Claude Amiel

THE VENDOME PRESS

First published in the United States of America in 2005 by
The Vendome Press
1334 York Avenue, New York, NY 10021

Originally published by Editions du Chêne—Hachette Livre as
Maisons d'artistes.

Copyright © 2004 Editions du Chêne—Hachette Livre

English translation copyright © 2005 The Vendome Press

Frederic Church's Olana photographed by Paul Rocheleau

First printing

ISBN:978-0-86565-276-7

Book design by Sandrine Bouet

English translation by Barbara Mellor

Library of Congress Cataloging-in-Publication Data
Lemaire, Gérard-Georges.
 [Maisons d'artistes. English]
 Artists' houses / by Gérard-Georges Lemaire ; photography by
Jean-Claude Amiel.
    p. cm.
 Translation of: Maisons d'artistes.
 ISBN 0-86565-230-9 (alk. paper)
 1. Artists—Europe—Homes and haunts. 2. Artists—United States—
Homes and haunts. I. Amiel, Jean-Claude. II. Title.
 N6754.L46 2004
 700'.92'2--dc22
                                2004049636

Printed in China

Contents

Top
Rembrandt's house in Amsterdam.

Above
Villa Böcklin, Fiesole.

Preface

Artists' houses that have survived the vicissitudes of history and the neglect of time more or less intact are all too rare. This is particularly sad because of the wealth of precious clues these homes can offer, both to the individual lives they have witnessed and—more generally—to changes in the social status of artists through the centuries. From them we can learn how their occupants lived, how they worked, and how they presented themselves to the world around them, both as individuals and artists.

The Renaissance saw a fundamental change in the image of the artist in society, in a return to the privileged status that had been the artist's due in ancient Greece and Rome, but which had been eclipsed in the medieval period. Writers such as Leon Battista Alberti began to make references to artists' living quarters and to their studios. The *studiolo,* we learn from Leonardo da Vinci, became the focus (indeed sometimes, as in Gubbio, the tangible expression) of the latest ideas in science and technology. Unfortunately, surviving examples of the living conditions of these geniuses of the Renaissance are rare. Andrea Mantegna's house in Padua still stands, with a floor plan indicative of social ambition, from a *casa degli artificali* (house of simulacra) to a *casa dei nobili* (house of the nobility). Piero della Francesca's house at Borgo San Sepolcro bears witness to the substantial enlargements that the artist carried out on the old dwelling that he had bought. The austere exterior of the Casa Buonarroti on Via Ghibellina in Florence conceals treasures within in the form of wall paintings exalting the family of Michelangelo, painted by the illustrious artist's great-nephew Michelangelo Buonarroti the Younger. The Venetian residence of Jacopo Tintoretto, as depicted in a lithograph by Marco Comirato, testifies to the spectacular success that enabled him to live in this small palazzo overlooking the Rio de la Sensa. Dürer ended his days in a handsome dwelling in Nuremberg, and El Greco's Toledo residence, with its splendid patio, spoke eloquently of his success. The Mannerist painter Federico Zuccaro designed the facade of the Palazzo Zuccaro in Rome as a grotesque face, with a gaping mouth for its front door, and the interior decorations were equally singular, featuring eccentric stucco work, frescoes, grotesques, and painted ceilings. Perhaps the ultimate example of this desire on artists' part to transform their dwellings into expressions of their artistic vision is to be found in the Casa Vasari in Arezzo, where a succession of large wall paintings bears graphic witness to the taste and learning of the author of *Lives of the Artists*.

In the early seventeenth century, the wealthy and influential Peter-Paul Rubens was in a position not only to run his own studio employing numerous assistants and specialist painters, but also to build a large residence set in an equally large garden. Half of this imposing building was in contemporary Flemish style, while the other half was like a palace housing his vast art collection, with his finest classical sculptures displayed in a hall inspired by the Pantheon in Rome. Rembrandt possessed an equally impressive collection in his Amsterdam house, known to us from the inventories drawn up in response to his crippling financial problems.

Here and there over the centuries we also find the ostentatious signs of material success, such as the magnificent *hôtel particulier* in Paris chosen by Charles Lebrun and his wife as their marital home following their belated reconciliation, or the Quinta del Sordo, a country house on the outskirts of Madrid bought by Francisco de Goya in 1819, where he displayed his large paintings such as *Saturn* and *Judith and Holofernes*.

In the nineteenth century the image of the artist underwent another transformation, becoming more diverse, polarized, even paradoxical. While some lived the bohemian lifestyle that took its name from Henri Murger's *Scènes de la vie de bohème*, others devoted themselves to forging solid reputations and equally solid fortunes. Eugène Delacroix had a studio built to his own design on Place Furstemberg, while Théodore Géricault preferred the new district of Nouvelle Athènes in northern Paris. Successful academic painters lived in lavish apartments or mansionlike *hôtels particuliers*, complete with spacious and elegant studios where they could receive their distinguished clients. Ary Scheffer, Alfred Stevens, and Jean-Léon Gérôme lived and worked in sumptuous style in Paris; in London Lord Leighton built his magnificent villa with its astonishing Arab hall as its center-piece; Arnold Böcklin built a lavish house in Zurich, dividing

his time between this and a Renaissance-style villa in Fiesole; and Franz von Stuck built the palace of his dreams in Munich. More avant-garde artists, by contrast, were more or less social outcasts and found themselves condemned to live in far less prestigious surroundings. Most of the Impressionist painters were not cushioned by any private income and lived in modest circumstances, as may be seen in Jean-François Millet's house at Barbizon.

Increasingly artists sought to invest their homes with some kind of emblematic significance. Francesco Paolo Michetti turned the convent building in which he lived at Francavilla Mare into a meeting place for the most eminent artists and intellectuals of his time, including Gabriele d'Annunzio, Matilde Serao, and Totsi. For others it was the gardens they created that became a major source of inspiration, as with Henri le Sidaner at Gerberoy, Pierre Bonnard at Le Cannet, and especially Claude Monet at Giverny. Others viewed their living quarters merely as temporary extensions of their studio space, places of passing significance that could be reduced to the bare essentials, as in Vincent van Gogh's *Bedroom* and *Chair*, painted during his time in Arles in 1888. Yet others—as though to emphasize that the new approach to painting was accompanied by a new approach to living— fostered nomadic tendencies, seeking their subject matter in nature (as at Fontainebleau, Barbizon, Pont-Aven, and the Mediterranean) or under distant skies (such as William Holman Hunt's tent, pitched in the desert by the Dead Sea; Frederick Lewis's Moorish house in Cairo; or Paul Gauguin's legendary studio-house, La Maison du Jouir, at Atuona in the Marquesas islands in 1902).

With the explosion of modern art in the early twentieth century, the possible (and occasionally impossible) permutations for artists' living arrangements multiplied exponentially, whether they were experiments in communal living as at Le Bateau-Lavoir and La Ruche; artists' colonies as at Murnau in Bavaria or Laethem-Saint-Martin in Flanders; pure utopias in which the artist's home became a work in itself, as with Dalí at Cadaquès and Hundertwasser in Vienna; or utopian fictions, as in the different incarnations of Kurt Schwitters's Merzbau.

ANDRÉ DERAIN

Opposite
André Derain's studio as he left it in 1954.

Above
Derain's acquisition of his country estate at Chambourcy marked an abrupt and far-reaching change in his life. Turning his back on fashionable society and the trappings of success, he abandoned most of his friends and became a recluse. Chambourcy was the gilded cage in which he was to remain until his death, leaving only during the war when it was looted by soldiers of the Wehrmacht on their inexorable advance through France in 1940. Blacklisted after the Liberation, he found solace there with a few close friends, subsequently finding the strength to explore new avenues in his art, particularly in the realm of sculpture.

Top right
André Derain.

In 1901, André Derain (1880–1954) and his friend Maurice Vlaminck discovered the work of Vincent van Gogh. It was a revelation, prompting them to experiment with new tech niques and the bold use of color that was to make them, with their older colleague Henri Matisse, the chief protagonists of fauvism. In 1905 their works provoked an outcry at the Salon des Indépendants. Two years later, inspired by Cézanne, Derain turned to cubism, becoming a pioneer of the movement with works such as his *Bathers* (1907). Instead of following Braque and Picasso in their pursuit of synthetic cubism, however,he gradually developed his own highly individual form of figurative art, inspired on occasion by neoclassicism, but more often by the new geometrical understanding of pictorial space. By the 1920s his reputation was at its height, and he embarked on a number of successful designs for theatrical and dance productions—a passion that was to remain with him for the rest of his life. Then quite suddenly he withdrew from Paris and fashionable society, broke off relations with most of his friends and family, and went to live in seclusion in a country house that he had bought at Chambourcy. There he spent fifteen years in the wilderness.

"Any artist who cannot add a bird to a landscape has no sense of the infinite … "
André Derain, manuscript in the Bibliothèque Doucet.

The internal exile of André Derain

In 1935, Derain made a decision that influenced the rest of his life. Having gotten rid of all his other properties—the house that he had built in the Parc Montsouris for himself and Georges Braque, the château at Parouzeau, and another house at Chailly-en-Brière—he bought "La Roseraie," a handsome late-seventeenth-century country house at Chambourcy, not far from Saint-Germain-en-Laye. Privacy was assured by extensive grounds embellished with statues, a lake, a magnificent rose garden, and an array of eighteenth-century follies including the Temple of Love, complete with stained-glass windows. To these amenities the artist added, according to his niece Geneviève Taillade, "a vegetable garden, a tennis court, and an orangery, which he used for large-scale paintings." Other features included a boat with a thatched canopy, brought there by the previous owners, and a menagerie of cats, dogs, peacocks, and a pair of goats roaming the lawns.

Abruptly, Derain renounced every aspect of his life in Paris, severing all contacts with his circle of acquaintances, and even with Vlaminck, his close companion in the early years at Chatou and up to the outbreak of the First World War. This sudden and radical change on Derain's part came shortly after the death of his agent, Paul Guillaume, which caused him great distress. But was this the reason why he became a recluse? He was after all at the pinnacle of his career, with a major exhibition at the Durand-Ruel gallery in New York only two years earlier, and another at A. Tooth & Sons in London.

His career continued largely as before, with more exhibitions in Paris, Stockholm, and London, and a retrospective of his work at the Kunsthalle in Basel. He designed the costumes and sets for *Salade,* by Albert Flament and Darius Milhaud, performed at the Palais Garnier. The Swiss publisher Albert Skira commissioned him to illustrate Rabelais's *Pantagruel.* But he devoted most of his time to painting the landscapes of the Île-de-France, and in the years that followed he also made increasingly frequent trips to Brittany to paint. While continuing to produce designs for the theater and ballet and holding exhibitions throughout Europe, he was actually devoting himself to these private, hidden projects. Then in 1938 he became fascinated once more by sculpture, working mostly in clay to create painted masks of ancient or primitive inspiration.

These years of seclusion were nonetheless a prolific time for Derain. The still lifes on a black ground that he painted have an extraordinary power, and history paintings such as *The Clearing* and *The Return of Ulysses* are even more remarkable. He also painted beautiful nude studies in a unique style informed by his wide experience of both fauvism and cubism. Although he continued to shun Paris society, he now received close friends including François Carco, Blaise Cendrars, Pierre Reverdy, Balthus (who in 1936 painted his portrait), Henri Sauguet, Jean Renoir, and Alberto Giacometti, who was one of his greatest admirers.

Below

A drawing done by Derain as a sketch for a sculpture. Toward the end of his life he found renewed inspiration in primitive art, especially for his sculpture.

"Derain has a supernatural gift for making things—give him a tin kettle and in half a morning he will hammer you out a Sumerian head; he has the fingers of a pianist, aptitude that brings beauty to life with a turn of the wrist; in a word, that sensibility of touch which keeps an ordinary craftsman happy for a lifetime—and these things terrify him. He ties both hands behind his back and fights so. Deliberately he chooses the most commonplace aspects and the most unlovely means of expression, hoping that, talent thus bound, genius will be stung into action."
Clive Bell, "The Authority of M. Derain," in *Since Cézanne*, Chatto and Windus, London, 1922.

Right
At Chambourcy in the last phase of his life, Derain's passion for sculpture was revived, and he produced a large number of works inspired by classical art and by the art of Africa and the South Pacific.

Below
Paints and brushes in the artist's studio.

Opposite
The Artist and his Family, André Derain, c.1939. In 1939 Derain was approaching his sixtieth birthday. That year he exhibited in America, and not in France. Raymonde Knaubliche, his model and mistress of some years, had a son by him, André, known as Bobby. This predominantly black self-portrait encapsulates his view of both his work and his private life at this time. In his domestic life he was surrounded by women and animals, both familiar and exotic. On the table, meanwhile, stands a fruit bowl with fruit, a simple and modest composition that embodied his notion of the ideal subject for art.

"The classical world sought only to represent ideas. Any feeling that could not find its own physical form did not exist, but was merely an illusion or a superstition. Cannot these forms conjure up the reality of that same feeling today? How could we understand anything if the way in which it was represented was constantly changing? We have to submit to the requirements of our inheritance. The cardinal role of art lies precisely in its ability to touch the soul directly through an object that represents an idea. Imagine for a moment what it would be like if we were forever calling the alphabet into question and redefining it— we would lose our means of reading, writing, even thinking."

"André Derain in his own words, collected by Gaston Diehl," *Peintres d'aujourd'hui, les Maîtres,* **Collection Comoedia Charpentier, Paris, June 10, 1943.**

Below
Decorative objects in the studio.

Opposite
On the studio wall, the shadow cast by a model boat belonging to Derain.

"More than Picasso, perhaps, Derain is aware that tradition lost all its rights when it found no echoes in the contemporary spirit. In spite of this, he takes greater delight than Picasso in teetering on the brink of the abyss of archaism and academicism."

Carlo Carrà, "Derain," in *Valori plastici,* 1924.

Though France stood on the brink of war, 1940 was not a bad year for Derain, with a one-man show at the Pierre Matisse Gallery in New York. But with the outbreak of war and the rapid German advance on Paris, he found himself forced to leave Chambourcy and sought refuge in Normandy and afterward, as events unfolded, in the Charente and the Ariège. By September Derain and his family were in Vichy, before going on to Aubusson, where he put the final touches to the tapestry of *The Hunt.* On October 1 he returned to Chambourcy, where he found his house had been looted and requisitioned by the German occupying forces, with many of his works and much of his furniture destroyed. Derain saved what he could, and was taken in by the village baker. Finally he returned to Paris, where he stayed with a friend before renting an apartment on the rue Huysmans. He continued to paint, seeking inspiration on the banks of the Loire and in the forest of Fontainebleau, but he no longer exhibited in France.

In November 1941, at the invitation of Arno Brecker, he went to Germany in a party of artists that also included Paul Belmondo, Vlaminck, Marcel Landowski, Kees van Dongen, Dunoyer de Segonzac, and Othon Friez. In his pocket, as the train drew out of the Gare de l'Est, was a list of artists who had been deported, and whose freedom he vainly hoped to achieve. Traveling through Bavaria and Austria, he was moved at times to despair and at others to wonder. He sent a letter to his wife, Alice, on November 4, "I write to you from Vienna, a most beautiful city which I greatly regret not having visited before. We stayed in Munich, where we were received magnificently. I should say sumptuously, even. There I saw some extremely interesting works, some defying the imagination."

In 1943 he was able to reclaim his house at Chambourcy and complete major works. There he found peace once more, amid a decor that in the end was quite restrained and of classical inspiration. "The furniture," explains Taillade, "came from his former residence, which he had built on rue Douanier in Paris, opposite Braque. It consisted of early antique tables, sombre and austere, one of which came from a convent. These were complemented by numerous musical instruments, a fine Louis XV organ, a harmonium, a baby grand piano, an upright piano purchased from the estate of Erik Satie, and even a hunting horn from which it used to amuse Derain to try to extract a few notes."

After the Liberation, however, Derain faced serious problems because of his visit to the Third Reich. Summoned to an inquiry by the Comité d'épuration, he refused to appear. Though eventually cleared of charges of collaboration, he was ruthlessly ostracized and suffered greatly as a result. Shunning all contact with the authorities in power, he refused to sell any works to the state and did not show his work in Paris again until 1949.

Derain's studio at Chambourcy lay on the second floor, in a large bedroom lit by four windows that he enlarged by removing the veranda attached to the dining room. In contrast to the rest of the enormous house, this was a place of the imagination and of unruly and—according to its own idiosyncratic logic—carefully planned clutter. Here, surrounded by African masks (he had been one of the first people in Europe to perceive their aesthetic value), by his own masks, and by medieval statues, he worked on his paintings and sculptures, on his models for stage designs, and on his book illustrations and engravings. The orangery in the grounds, meanwhile, was converted into a studio for pieces on a larger scale, such as his Golden Age cycle, which he completed there in 1946.

Two years later, Jean Leymarie visited Chambourcy and observed, "One October morning in 1948 I find myself in the alchemist's laboratory, thronged with Bosch monstrosities, bronzes from Benin, Romanesque sculptures, Negro fetishes, and curiosities of folk art, all illumined by the magical light of Vlaminck's famous Congolese mask. The windows look out over the unchanging forest whose mystery he has tried so often to penetrate. Derain reveals the point of luminous white light by which objects are irradiated. The crucial thing for him is to find his precise place in painting. With rare simplicity and detachment he displays his most secret works, . . . accomplished improvised pieces full of freshness, or a large nude on which he has been working doggedly for the last twenty years. . . . 'My obsessions,' he confesses: 'Every artist has his prison.' . . . Sketches in progress, propped on the floor, catch me unawares with their new and sudden intensity. Studies for a large composition, probably a Dance. 'Without the human figure, nothing is certain,' explains Derain."

Derain painted his *Self-Portrait* in about 1953. It shows an old man defeated by life. The following year, after a long and painful illness affecting his sight, he was hit by a truck and died at Garches. As Derain lay on his deathbed, Alberto Giacometti, his most loyal disciple, asked him if there was anything he would like. "A piece of sky and a bicycle," came the reply.

Below
Terracotta sculptures
by Derain.

Opposite
Don Quixote and *Sancho
Panza*, two sculptures
by Derain.

"At first glance, swift and voracious, Derain's studio is the epitome of the romantic artist's garret. A world of danger? But so *sympathique!* So full of dust and cobwebs, lavish in the warmest of the sun's rays.... André Derain, who is not a romantic but who has a sense of drama and who, following trail after dramatically traced trail, has rediscovered the first of the paths of classicism to have been engulfed in the mists of academicism and the bogus fogs of scholarly posturing and diabolical pedantry..."
André Salmon, *André Derain, Les peintres français nouveaux no. 15,* Editions de la Nouvelle Revue Française, 1924.

BLOOMSBURY GROUP

Opposite
One of the many surfaces painted by Vanessa Bell:
a cupboard door in her own studio.

Above
In the summer of 1916, Vanessa Bell, urged on by her
sister Virginia Woolf, bought a small farmhouse called
Charleston, in the Sussex Downs near Lewes. There
she, the painter Duncan Grant, and the painter and
critic Roger Fry devoted themselves to their own work
and to the complete redecoration of every surface of
the house. Thus Charleston became not only the
aesthetic manifesto of the Bloomsbury Group, but
also the setting for the translation of their philosophy
of life into physical action. All the members of the
Bloomsbury Group—Lytton Strachey, John Maynard
Keynes, David Garnett, and of course Leonard and
Virginia Woolf—were frequent houseguests.

Top right
John Maynard Keynes (seated), Duncan Grant (left),
and Clive Bell (right) in Sussex in 1919.

Few coteries of intellectuals and writers have exercised so broad
an influence as the Bloomsbury Group in Britain in the first half
of the twentieth century. Clustered around the central figure of
Virginia Stephen (1882–1941), later to marry the publisher Leonard
Woolf (1880–1969), its members devoted their energies to
questioning the prevailing Victorian values that they had
inherited and to promoting the reform of social mores (especially
sexual freedom), of the political system, and of the economy.
Virginia's sister Vanessa (1876–1961), who married the art critic
Clive Bell (1881–1964), set out meanwhile to bring about a similar
revolution in the art world. With her friends Duncan Grant
(1885–1978), himself an artist, and the painter and critic Roger Fry
(1866–1934), their senior in years and soon their mentor, they
formed a circle inspired by French artists from the impressionists
to Cézanne and Matisse. When Vanessa Bell moved with her
family to Charleston, she devoted herself, with the aid of Grant
and Fry, to decorating every surface in the house. There she set up
a way of life and a style of education for her children that were to
typify the spirit of Bloomsbury. Charleston itself became a
constantly changing work of art, with all the rooms and the
contents painted by Bell, Fry, and Grant in a manner that reflected
their whole philosophy, a combination of ethics and aesthetics
unshackled by doctrine or dogma. Yet Charleston never became
a museum piece or a grand memorial to the Bloomsbury Group,
but has always remained the simple, everyday setting for an
artistic vision that ran counter to the "Englishness" of British art.

An aesthetic utopia at Charleston

The names of the two Stephen sisters, Virginia and Vanessa, occupy a prominent place in the pantheon of early twentieth-century culture in Britain. Virginia married the writer and publisher Leonard Woolf, while Vanessa married the art historian and critic Clive Bell. The novels of Virginia Woolf now stand as masterpieces of the Edwardian era, and Vanessa Bell's paintings are the purest expression of British post-impressionism. Both of them rejected wholesale the spirit of Victorian England, favoring instead a radical transformation of social and familial relationships, and particularly the emancipation of women and a revolution in sexual attitudes.

While the Stephens grew up in Bloomsbury (from which the group that started to form around them from 1905 took its name), near the British Museum, the outbreak of the First World War prompted them to look for a country retreat for the summer months. After Leonard and Virginia married, the couple moved into a Regency house near Asheham in the Ouse valley where Virginia wrote her early novels. Her sister came with her husband and Duncan Grant for weekend house parties, which also often included the economist John Maynard Keynes and the essayist Lytton Strachey, who wrote the opening chapters of *Eminent Victorians* there. Soon the Woolfs moved to Rodmell, on the other side of the river, where they lived in Monk's House, a cottage that was to be a haven of peace for Virginia. John Lehmann has described how after eating in an upstairs room overlooking the garden, with its orchard on one side and its goldfish pond on the other, she would sit beside the fire smoking strong cigarettes that she rolled herself and talking.

Virginia tried to persuade her sister to follow her example and look for a house in Sussex, writing to her in 1916, "I want you to leave Wissett and take Charleston," adding that she believed Vanessa could make it "absolutely divine." Certainly the author of *Jacob's Room* had an unusual talent for discovering remarkable houses; this eighteenth-century farmhouse on the edge of the South Downs, not far from Asheham, boasted not only a large walled garden and a lake, but also a small cottage on the grounds to accommodate guests.

For Vanessa Bell it was love at first sight, and in October 1916 she visited it again with her children, her lover Duncan Grant, and the writer David Garnett, who was lover to them both. She confided excitedly to her friend Roger Fry, "It's most lovely, very solid and simple, with . . . perfectly flat windows and wonderful tiled roofs. The pond is most beautiful, with a willow at one side and a stone or flint wall edging it all round the garden part, and a little lawn sloping down to it, with formal bushes on it." She was not blind to the fact that it would require a lot of work and that the wallpapers were frightful, but she was determined, "It will be an odd life, but . . . it ought to be a good one for painting." Redecorating the house, as it turned out, was to be a lifelong passion for her. Vanessa decorated it in the style that was typical of the Bloomsbury Group, often appealing to her friends, according to Angelica Garnett (her daughter with Duncan Grant who was born at Charleston and eventually married David Garnett), to help her transform it into a spiritual refuge and a haven from the harshest aspects of the outside world. Vanessa applied herself to the decorations, while David Garnett and Duncan Grant (who were working there as conscientious objectors) took charge of the farm and livestock. Roger Fry, concerned by Vanessa's announcement that she intended to set up a small school for her children, rushed back to London to find a servant and a governess or private tutor. Eventually he overcame his misgivings and did all he could to help her bring her idea to fruition.

In the matter of aesthetics, the artists and critics of the Bloomsbury Group believed that all modern creativity should take a root-and-branch critique of British art as its starting point. They were determined at all costs to save British art from its own insularity. Roger Fry played a crucial role in forming the group and defining its aims. After working at the Metropolitan Museum of Art in New York, this brilliant art historian decided to become an independent painter. He had in mind the launch of a movement for which he coined the name "post-impressionism," a highly personal conception of the nature of art that owed a great deal to Cézanne, the fauvists, and the cubists. The Grafton Galleries in London asked him to curate a major exhibition of French art, from Degas to Picasso, which attracted a great deal of

A nude by Duncan Grant on an easel in the studio where he worked until a few days before his death at the age of ninety-three.

"Duncan, like a sailor, was always quietly occupied by a task of his own invention. 'Creative activity was his passion—he was never satisfied with what he had ready-made—he longed to make something new.' Those words written of Chekhov were equally true of Duncan.... In his schemes Duncan was always seconded by Vanessa—they painted together in harmony, perfectly happy while they were at work, and rarely resting from it. Thus Charleston was transformed."
David Garnett, *The Flowers of the Forest*, 1955.

Duncan Grant's studio as he
left it in 1977 with his library,
his collection of paintings
(mostly by fellow members of
the Bloomsbury Group), and his
ceramics.

"The half-finished canvases by Duncan Grant, or Julian's mother, Vanessa, or his brother Quentin, piled carelessly in the studios, and the doors and fireplaces of the old farmhouse transformed by decorations of fruit and flowers and opulent nudes by the same hands, the low square tables made of tiles fired in Roger Fry's Omega Workshops, and the harmony created all through the house by the free, brightly colored, Post-Impressionist style that one encountered in everything, from the huge breakfast cup one drank one's coffee from to the bedroom curtains that were drawn in the morning, not by a silent-footed valet or housemaid but by one's own hand to let in the Sussex sunshine . . . "

John Lehmann, *Whispering Gallery*, 1955.

Left
A bust of Vanessa Bell on the chest of drawers in Duncan Grant's studio.

Above (two pictures)
Photographs and drawings of familiar figures from the Bloomsbury Group, including Vanessa Bell (top), on the mantelpiece in Grant's studio.

"I wish you wouldn't always do your best thing just to decorate an odd corner of your house."

Roger Fry, letter to Vanessa Bell, Brittany, early September 1920.

Duncan Grant decorated
every surface of the fireplace
in his studio, an eclectic room
with its furniture chosen
principally for comfort.

"At Charleston it was our habit to sit after dinner in an oblate semicircle before
a curious fireplace, devised and constructed by Roger Fry to heat with logs a
particularly chilly room; strange to say, it did. Each of us would be reading his
or her book, and someone was sure to be reading French."
Clive Bell, *Old Friends*, 1956.

"Charleston is by no means a gentleman's house, I bicycled there in a flood of rain & found the baby asleep in its cot, & Nessa & Duncan sitting over the fire, with bottles & bibs & basins all around them. Duncan went to make my bed....
One has the feeling of living on the brink of a move. In one of the little islands of comparative order Duncan set up his canvas, & Bunny [David Garnett] wrote a novel in a set of copy books. Nessa scarcely leaves the babies, or if she appears for a moment outside, she has instantly to go off ... to wash napkins, or bottles, or prepare meals ..."
Virginia Woolf, *Diaries,* **March 5, 1919.**

Portrait of a Model, Vanessa Bell, 1913. At this period Vanessa Bell was also producing more avant-garde work, even embracing abstraction in 1915, along with Duncan Grant. The numerous landscapes she painted at Charleston indicated her desire to return to the more restrained world of post-impressionism, as envisaged by Roger Fry from 1910.

"There was only one thing I didn't like at Charleston—need you do so much housework? Because the bloody government has made slaves of Duncan and Bunny [David Garnett], need it make one of you? And why don't you paint more?"
Clive Bell, letter to Vanessa Bell, December 1916.

attention, and it was through this event that he met Vanessa and Clive Bell, rapidly becoming their mentor. The following year he organized another exhibition at the Grafton Galleries, this time devoted to modernist art in France and Britain. The shows shook the British art establishment to its foundations, to the great excitement of younger artists, as Duncan Grant remembered: "It was really a moment which brought together all the younger painters in England into a sort of mass movement. They agreed that something had happened that they must cope with and I think that is what led eventually to the Omega."

The Omega Workshops opened in July 1913 when Roger Fry decided to launch a campaign to redirect working artists away from pure art and toward the applied arts. To this end he set up an agency for the production of a wide range of items, which would be the expression of the Bloomsbury aesthetic. The project was utopian in nature, with the objects manufactured in its workshops remaining anonymous and the artists receiving a regular wage to enable them to devote themselves to their own work. Roger Fry explained his beliefs in his preface to the Omega catalogue: "The artist is the man who creates not only for need but for joy, and in the long run mankind will not be content without sharing that joy through the possession of real works of art, however humble or unpretentious they may be." Wyndham Lewis, the young French sculptor Henri Gaudier-Brzeska, David Bomberg, Jessie and Frederick Etchells, Duncan Grant, and Vanessa Bell all took part in the new experiment, producing furniture, ceramics, and textiles, among many other things.

Charleston became the embodiment of the Omega Workshops ideal. But as well as being the expression of this democratic aesthetic, it was above all a highly specific lifestyle, eccentric and gently subversive. Adopting a number of existential and educational precepts inspired by the writings of Rousseau, Vanessa and the others lived according to the principle of the freedom of the individual, limited only by the need to respect the freedom of others.

Although she shared her sister's ideals, Virginia was sometimes disconcerted by her sister's insouciant approach, blissfully unconcerned as she was at overstepping the bounds of even the most basic decencies, "Nessa is four miles on the other side of the down, living like an old hen wife among ducks, chickens, and children. She never wants to put on proper clothes again—even a bath seems to distress her. Her children are forever asking her questions and she invents all sorts of answers, never having known very accurately about facts." Virginia was astonished that amid all this chaos—disarmingly picturesque as it undoubtedly was—her younger sister should somehow contrive to look after the farmyard and the schoolroom, manage a *ménage à trois* or even *à quatre,* and still find time to devote herself not only to her own painting, but also to covering every square inch of the house in a different color. Between her frequent visits to London, where she had a studio, and her trips abroad, Vanessa worked incessantly to make her country retreat even more delightful. Having painted the chimney breast and the two doors to either side of it in Duncan Grant's room, she gradually transformed every room in the house. The finishing

touches were works produced by these artists during the 1920s and 30s, especially fabrics and numerous ceramics designed by Duncan Grant. Vanessa Bell's style, like Grant's, became ever looser, simpler, and more flowing. Increasingly they favored mythological subjects, which they treated in a lyrical, distant manner, imbued with great freedom and a playful gaiety.

Every room was filled with glowing fabrics and exotic objects brought back from travels through France, Italy, Greece, and Turkey, in addition to the wealth of objects created by Bell, Fry, and Grant. They let their imaginations run loose on the painted furniture, and arranged the interiors and chose colors for dramatic effect, creating an atmosphere of peaceful harmony and gentle eccentricity. The crockery, meanwhile, came from the Omega Workshops. Paradoxically, this was a harmony that owed nothing to any unity of either style or concept. On the contrary, it emerged from an extraordinary eclecticism. Only Vanessa Bell's bedroom (later turned into a library) displayed a measure of homogeneity, forming a stark contrast to the other rooms, which were in a perpetual state of decorative flux.

In 1939 Charleston underwent major alterations, changing both its appearance and its atmosphere. The bedrooms were arranged differently and Bell and Grant decided to add some of their paintings from their respective London studios. Clive Bell, meanwhile, added his superb collection of French paintings. Charleston now took on the appearance of a small but exceptional gallery of modern art, with British post-impressionist works rubbing shoulders with drawings and canvases by old and modern masters in a charmingly arbitrary fashion. A similarly happy lack of discipline reigned in the library, which contained precious volumes and first editions of the works of Byron, Voltaire, Pepys, and T. S. Eliot, alongside—naturally—the works of the Bloomsbury writers, all published by Leonard Woolf's Hogarth Press. Nothing was to appear fixed or unchangeable; everything was to be part of a present that was in a constant state of flux and change. Life, with all its necessary whims and caprices, was the sole arbiter and genius loci of this lovely old farmhouse, with all its eccentricities and its exhilarating and exuberant decorations.

"Vanessa presided in the dining-room, the magnetic center of all our thoughts and activities. At breakfast she was always down first and sat for some time alone, enjoying her solitude. She had dressed and washed quietly, almost secretively, and would be at her habitual place on the far side of the round table, looking with dreamy reflection at the still-life in the center, or out of the window at the pond and the weather."

Angelica Garnett, *Deceived with Kindness*, 1984.

Above
Portrait of Zoum van den Eeckhoudt, Roger Fry, 1915.

"The only drawbacks seemed to be that there is cold water, and not hot, in the bathroom; not a very nice WC . . ."
Virginia Woolf, letter to Vanessa Bell, Corbis Bay, Cornwall, Sunday, September 24, 1916.

"Nessa seems to have slipped civilization off her back, and splashes about entirely nude, without shame, and with enormous spirit. Indeed, Clive now takes the line that she has ceased to be a presentable lady. I think it all works admirably."
Virginia Woolf on Vanessa Bell at Charleston, c. 1916.

Below

The garden room, with walls stenciled by Vanessa Bell and chimney breast painted by Duncan Grant. Grant also designed the fish rug. On the wall hangs Bell's famous self-portrait, painted in 1958.

"He is so incredibly full of charm, his genius as an artist seems to overflow so into his life and character and he is so amusing too and odd and unaccountable."
Vanessa Bell on Duncan Grant, March 7, 1937.

Right
František Bílek in his summer studio at Chynov, a cottage he created with great care, and which was a reflection of his intimate connection with the culture of Bohemia. In his view, the city of Prague was "pandemonium," and he built his main residence, a villa, as a sanctuary, where art would serve a mystical—and hence redemptive—vision of the world.

FRANTIŠEK BÍLEK

Opposite
The dining room on the first floor with furniture and decorations—including an ironwork chandelier inspired by oak leaves—designed by Bílek.

Above (two pictures)
The Bílek villa, close to the Belvedere in Prague. Bílek drew up the plans and designed the decorative scheme, inside and out.

Forced to give up his art studies in Paris before he could complete a two-year scholarship, František Bílek (1872–1941) returned to his native Bohemia (now the Czech Republic) and set up his studio in the woods at Chynov. Here in 1898 he built a cottage, drawing up the plans himself in order to be certain that the studio met his needs as a sculptor, and was in harmony with both his religious beliefs and his mystical love of nature. On the facade he sculpted a bas-relief of a kneeling woman changing her infant child, accompanied by the inscription "We are protected." This innovative building is generally regarded as the earliest example of Secessionist architecture. Later, when Bílek moved to Prague, he again designed his own house, which he hoped would provide a refuge from the intellectual and political arguments raging in the world outside. To him it was a temple on earth, which formed part of a highly complex spiritual and symbolic plan. Adapting the ideas of religion and nature explored in his sculptures to his villa and studio, Bílek created a structure simultaneously bound to the earthly world by its power and passion, and in close harmony with the mystical nature of the divine. This duality in Bílek's philosophy is expressed in every element of the architecture and decoration, from the plan to the furniture and even the door hinges, all made to his own design.

In Bilek's studio some of his large-scale sculptures can be viewed from above through round-arched windows resembling those of a loggia. During the first decade of the twentieth century Bilek's work underwent a major transformation that would become the distinctive hallmark of his vision; his depictions of human figures became wracked by overwhelming and often agonizing emotion expressed through highly dramatic poses and gestures. The female figure of Woe (Indian wood, 1909), her long garment fastened at the chest by a large fibula, clutches her head with one hand and her breast with the other, her eyes closed. All Bilek's other standing female figures were carved in this same tortured spirit, together creating tragedies in three dimensions. In this period, Bilek abandoned all explicit reference to Christianity, preferring to create his own private religious iconography.

Right
The studio door designed by Bílek.

Far right
A view of the studio showing some of Bílek's most memorable works: his sculpture is characterized by a strong element of pathos and a preference for natural materials, especially wood, whether carved or left in its natural state.

František Bílek's sanctuary in Prague

It was only by default that the young František Bílek turned to sculpture, having been forced by color blindness to give up his study of painting at the Prague Academy of Fine Art in 1887. He then enrolled in the sculpture program at the School of Decorative Arts, where his conspicuous talent earned him a two-year stipend to study in Paris. In 1891, encouraged by the circle of Czech artists in Paris (including Alphonse Mucha), he enrolled in the Académie Colarossi. Unsatisfied, he soon left and continued drawing and sculpting on his own. During this time Bílek completed the sculpture *Golgotha,* which caused controversy in two ways: first, by depicting a starving and broken Christ rather than the romantic ideal, and second, by using real wire and rope as material. The unorthodox sculpture angered the stipend board and they revoked Bílek's placement, forcing him to return to Chynov.

Back in his native home, humiliated, this son of a wheel maker found inspiration in the forest of an old firing range and began to discover his talent for architecture when he drew up plans for his house and studio on the lot. Eventually, he left the isolated woods for the capital city of Prague, keeping his house in Chynov as a peaceful summer workshop. He obtained a plot abutting the castle walls in Prague where he could build another house and studio. Bílek viewed moving to the city with trepidation, "This pandemonium, this constant din, this frantic scurrying of people swept along by guilt and curses, my passion and the poverty made me weep and pray for our salvation." Determined at all costs to re-create in the city the peace and tranquility that he had enjoyed in his retreat at Chynov, he conceived an idea for an "ideal" dwelling; he wrote to a friend, "I want to build with my own hands a new temple—a temple of the kingdom of heaven on earth."

In 1910 he sketched out the first rough plans, and two years later he was able to move in, even though work was not quite finished. In January 1912 he admitted to a friend, "As yet I have no staircase; in August I shall bring back some ladders from Bůla, just in case. After all, as long as we are young we can manage without a staircase." As with the house he designed at Chynov, the facade was in traditional brick, though this did not prevent him from using concrete for the roof and supporting columns. Also as at Chynov, the architecture suggested the movements and surges of the soul. In his view architecture should "imitate nature in a language comprehensible by our brothers." This sacred mission rested on the conviction that "art is the handwriting through which we transcribe nature." This deep-seated naturalism was a metaphor for the reconciliation of the human world and the divine, with nature forming the connection between the two, or—better still—their fusion at a profound level. It was a cause of immense regret to him that this sacred connection had been broken, "We have not chosen the life of nature, we have not responded positively to the generous call of life through the medium of nature; rather we have responded with a challenge even more brazen than that of the Tower of Babel—we have hurled the dregs of human taste in the face of the Supreme Being."

The structure rests on oval-shaped foundations in order to accommodate the sloping nature of the site and is remarkable above all for its completely flat roof, unique in Prague. The east-facing facade is curved and extended by an ellipse containing Bílek's great statue of Moses, a masterpiece bought by the city of Prague in 1934 (The sculpture was destroyed by the Nazis in 1940 but recast from the original mold in 1945.) The three remaining facades of the house are flat and embellished with powerful Egyptian columns, truncated where they do not function as supports for the roof. Bílek chose the art of the ancient Egyptians as his influence because he believed their land was the privileged backdrop to the Bible. His two great entrance columns have been interpreted as references to Jakin and Boaz, the twin pillars of the Temple of Solomon in Jerusalem.

He perceived the white colonnade as embodying growth and life, as he explained in 1912: "Life is like a field of ripe corn offering our fellow men their daily bread. As its central axis the structure has a large statue—Moses, prophet of the Old Testamant—towards which it leans like a field of corn. Numerous ears gathered together in sheaves, form the pillars. Some of these are unfinished as they support nothing." For Bílek's friend, the poet Otokar Brezina, author of "The Apotheosis of Corn," a cornfield was both refuge and home, "What goodness! Fraternally, you have allowed him to dream of a summer of celestial beauty, alone, hidden among your serried rows." Bílek also introduced the theme of the

Three of the highly symbolic beech wood figures that make up the monumental group of *Future Conquerors*, subtitled *Allegory of the Seven Spiritual Senses* (1931–1937). The dramatic aesthetic Bílek adopted once he started working in Prague remained virtually unchanged over the next 30 years; by contrast, his relationship with the materials he used, already complex and profound, was to become even richer in his combinations of different materials and his use of color. In some ways Bílek revisited the Baroque tradition and adapted it to his own purposes, moving his figures through three dimensions, and with his group sculptures using space in such a way that the physical, emotional, and spiritual relationships between the figures unfolded with a pathos in which mystical transports mingled with sensuality. His respect for the human figure owed more to the Middle Ages than to any other period, and in his sculptures anatomical realism contributed to transforming his figures into images of the sublime.

In the center of the artist's studio stands one of his most famous sculptures, *Amazement* (beech, 1907). Bílek chose to leave the walls of the studio in bare stone, which reinforced the relationship that he felt between the materials he used—principally wood (in which he prized to the point of exaggeration the qualities of different species), and painted plaster. Also in stone, the large arch connecting the two sides of the studio was carried in from a local ruin and expresses Bílek's nationalism.

"Can a nation live without spiritual art? No! Clearly there is a reason why our nation cannot be awakened! It should devote its life and energies to the work it left off five hundred years ago, for the good of humanity and in the spirit of art!"
František Bílek, *Posthumous Writings.*

Below
A sculpture in Bilek's studio. In his view, sculpture expressed life, and life was manifested through form, volume, and color.

"All things foreign have not taken a good hold in our country. Their descent upon our environment was unnaturally violent and hard. They bring us monsters and diseases."
František Bílek, 1920.

Right
The entrance hall and staircase with an eclectic pillar designed by Bílek, making reference to numerous styles but conforming to none. The underlying coherence of the architecture of the Villa Bilek rests on a metaphysical vision rather than a stylistic approach. Bilek borrowed from medieval art, making free use of stained glass, while constantly introducing other references in wholly original juxtapositions. The result is a dualism between syncretism and solid coherence. Although they have little in common in terms of execution, his vision may be compared with Gaudí's.

Preceding pages
The dining room on the first floor with Bílek's doorframe in dressed stone with a carved lintel and column references.

Right and below
Hinges designed by Bílek. His strong attraction to the decorative arts is evident in every detail of this building. Equally clear is his outstanding degree of accomplishment in the applied arts, from his magnificent ironwork (of which the candelabra and the sophisticated decorative work on the furniture offer dazzling examples) to the austere but highly skilled construction of a doorframe in dressed stone with carved lintel and capitals. He also made stoneware vases in somber tones, darkened with lampblack, and decorated with plant motifs. Frequently he also added inscriptions to their irregular forms, so assigning them a place in the mystical mise-en-scène of his decorative scheme.

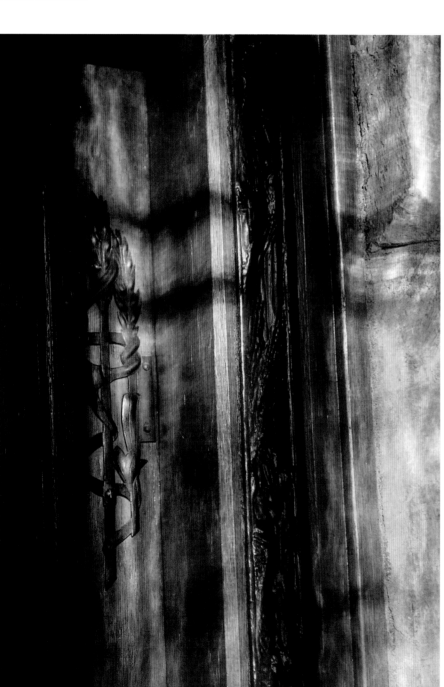

"Blessed be the lamb and he who sits on thorns; honor, glory and strength be to them for eternity."
Text engraved by František Bílek on his bookcase.

Bílek designed this dressing table (in solid birch, metal, and mirror glass) for his wife in 1911. The mirror takes the form of a book placed on a lectern. Bílek's designs for furniture are strictly spiritual in nature and do not conform to any formal theme. Conceived individually, each piece expresses an aspect of the artist's philosophy. They are mostly of light wood, sometimes with details in dark wood, as is seen here, and although Bílek sometimes delved into the repertoire of Czech folk art for his decorative motifs, he always simplified and transposed them.

"Our existence is a terrible dream towards the everlasting reality."
František Bílek, *The Persistence of the Human Body III, 1889.*

tree (most beloved of all to him), the acorn, and the oak leaf, developed on the exterior as well as the interior, in the decoration of the doors, on the frames, the panels, and the superb door hinges.

Balconies of varying dimensions project from the irregularly sized windows of Bílek's house, and a large terrace roofs a winter garden. Inside the threshold of the villa a passage runs off the hall to the dining room and the drawing room, with the doorways to various rooms arranged asymmetrically. As visitors penetrate deeper into the house the perspectives multiply, creating the impression of a profusion of different viewpoints, when in fact the arrangement of the rooms is relatively simple. Like the exterior of the building, the interior is characterized by an austere and unadorned simplicity of style, which is counterbalanced by the astonishingly inventive geometry and complex though discreet details of the decoration, designed to avoid "lifeless straight lines and irregular curves" and to favor more organic forms. For in Bílek's vision of the cosmos, "every natural movement of a line is a direct encouragement to life."

Bílek designed the elliptical staircase himself, as he did the door-knobs, the hinges, the stone doorframes, and the banisters. The small windows, meanwhile, were glazed with medieval stained glass. The furniture, also designed by Bílek, is notable for its extreme simplicity of form and for the painstaking attention given to chromatic contrasts and to decorative elements, which are never allowed to distract from the basic shape. A fine example is a horseshoe-shaped writing desk that he designed in 1906, which is decorated in relief with figurative scenes and a landscape and has inscriptions engraved on its pillars and curve, but retains an impeccable purity in its lines.

The southern part of the building, overlooking the Shatkov Sady gardens, contains the artist's private gallery and the studio. Extending the full height of the house, the studio allowed ample space for Bílek to work in and provided plenty of light from the many windows scattered throughout the room. A large-scale relief depicting the Ascension appears on the north facade. Our knowledge that this was the artist's earthly home and studio is overwhelmingly eclipsed by the sensation that the space is a religious sanctuary, an idiosyncratic temple intended to invoke a "dream of the voyage to the true life."

FREDERIC CHURCH

Left
The north sitting room of this Persian-inspired citadel overlooking the Hudson River Valley; Church designed the stencils and chose the colors for the walls and ceilings of the interior, as well as designing furniture to mix with family pieces, resulting in an oriental style combined with occidental touches.

Above
The facade of Olana, named after the treasure-house of a fortress in ancient Persia.

Top right
Frederic Church.

Frederic Edwin Church died in New York in 1900 at the age of seventy-four. Seven weeks after his death a major exhibition of his work opened to the public at the Metropolitan Museum of Art in New York; it was to be the last until the 1960s. During his lifetime Church was a celebrity among American painters; after his death he was forgotten for many years before his work began to return to favor. Today no book devoted to American art is complete without a discussion of his work, and his reputation is starting to spread to Europe. This long period in limbo—a fate he shared with many other nineteenth-century artists who were not members of any avant-garde movement—could so easily have proved fatal, not only to his paintings, but also to another great project that he undertook in parallel to his artistic work: the creation of his house and grounds at Olana in Hudson, New York, unique in both conception and style. Like Lord Leighton in London, Franz von Stuck in Munich, and Arnold Böcklin in Basel, Church set out to build a house that was both an expression of his aesthetic approach and a compendium of his life and spiritual aspirations. As he was principally a landscape artist, he also set out to transform the large estate that he put together over the years into a reflection of his world vision and his art.

Olana, a dreamlike citadel of Gothic and Oriental fantasy

The paintings of Frederic Edwin Church (1826–1900) are among the most striking produced in America in the nineteenth century. He had always been fascinated by the melodramatic compositions of the English artist John Martin and was a follower of Thomas Cole, who taught him from 1844 to 1846. Subsequently his paintings combine a strong romantic influence with a scientific curiosity typical of the encyclopedic spirit of his times and its epic quest for knowledge. This approach to art—the final legacy of the Renaissance—was swept aside by the advent of modern art, and is now unjustly associated with academicism.

Two events in the late 1850s changed the young artist's life forever. His painting *Niagara* (1857) was greeted with considerable acclaim, nationally and even internationally. And at the exhibition in which it hung he met Isabel Mortimer Carnes, whom he married in 1861. Church had already bought Wynson Breezy Farm, overlooking the Hudson River and surrounded by the Catskill Mountains, a spot to which Thomas Cole had introduced him and that inspired his first major painting, *Twilight among the Mountains (Catskill Creek),* exhibited at the National Academy of Design in 1845. He then decided to buy some land adjoining the farm and to build a new house at its furthest point. He gave the job of designing and building the house (which he nicknamed "Cosy Cottage") to the architect Richard Morris Hunt. In the spring of 1861, the newly married couple moved in. Their first two children, Herbert Edwin and Emma Frances, were born in the cottage. In celebration of their births Church painted *Sunrise* (for Herbert) and *Moonrise* (for Emma). The farm, with its fields of grain and its small farmyard, remained an important feature in his life. In about 1867, he built a large wooden studio on the heights of Long Hill, which offered magnificent views of the surrounding area. Now he also felt the need for a larger house, and asked Hunt to come up with ideas for a building resembling a French *manoir.* Over the years, Church also strove to remodel the surrounding countryside, transforming this classic arable landscape little by little into a purely ornamental farm. Inspired by the ideas of the Scottish garden designer Charles Smith, he was determined to fashion the entire estate into *vedute* in exactly the same way as if it were an artistic composition. This is not to imply that he neglected the agricultural side of the estate; on the contrary, he increased the area under cultivation, created kitchen gardens and flower gardens, and planted orchards and huge numbers of trees, either standing in isolation or in copses. To his friends he observed that "for several seasons after I selected this spot as my home, I thought of hardly anything but planting trees, and had thousands and thousands of them set out on the southern and northern slopes." The house itself was surrounded by apple trees. But this reshaping of the landscape through planting was not enough—he also redesigned the river banks and in 1873 excavated a lake.

Following the deaths of their two children in 1865, Frederic and Isabel decided to leave Olana for Jamaica, where he found inspiration for two of his masterpieces, *Rainy Season in the Tropics* and *The After Glow,* painted upon his return to Olana. Then after the birth of another son, Frederic Joseph in 1866, the family made a lengthy tour of Europe and the Mediterranean, spending time in London, where Church exhibited regularly and successfully; then going to Paris and Marseilles, where they embarked on a steamer to Alexandria. For several months they lived in Beirut, which Church found was "beautifully situated at the foot of a high range of mountains which are now snow clad, and the mountain sides are dotted all over with villages, convents, &c." He was especially captivated by the traditional architecture of the region, and this fascination for the ancient Orient was only increased by his visits to Petra and Jerusalem. Although several of his later paintings bore witness to this preoccupation, he never fell prey to the Orientalism that was then so much in vogue.

On his return to Olana in 1869 (after the birth of another son, Theodore Winthrop), his ideas for his future house had undergone a wholesale transformation. Although he did not altogether abandon the idea of a French *manoir,* he now envisaged something more akin to a citadel combining elements from Gothic revival and oriental architecture. Having fallen out with Hunt, who felt ill at ease with plans for a house that would be "Persian, adapted to the Occident," he turned to Calvert Vaux, with whom his relationship was not much happier as the two men could not agree on the aesthetic aims of the

Below
The dining hall and gallery with Church's collection of old master paintings.

"I hope to be in New York in a week or so—but a Feudal castle which I am building—under the modest name of a dwelling house—absorbs all my time and all my attention. I am obliged to watch it so closely—for having undertaken to get my architecture from Persia where I have never been—nor any of my friends either—I am obliged to imagine Persian architecture—then embody it on paper and explain it to a lot of mechanics whose ideal of architecture is wrapped up in felicitous recollections of a successful brick school house or meeting house or jail."
Frederic Church, letter to John Ferguson Weir, 1871.

The corridor leading to the studio. The strange mixture of elements coming from various cultures is dominated by an idea of medieval revival, which creates an odd but peaceful sensation of unity in spite of the diversity of the objects.

Below
One of the first-floor sitting rooms. Over the fireplace hangs *Sunset, Jamaica*, Frederic Church, 1865.

"I inaugurated the New Studio—it is perfect. Filled with enthusiasm I attacked my first canvas and an iceberg scene is the result, the best I think I ever painted and the truest."
Frederic Church, letter to Eastus Dow Palmer, 1891.

"I am indeed busy night and day with my plans and as I am architect and I make the drawings you can readily believe that I have little spare time. ... I wonder if I shall work as hard in the new Studio as I do in erecting it."
Frederic Church, letter to Charles De Wolf Brownell, 1888.

Right

Church's studio: he liked the idea of re-creating an oriental interior, but without precise references to a specific culture, even if the pieces of furniture are genuine.

Bottom

Church had the pilasters and arches in the main sitting room painted with vegetal motifs, while he left the rest of the decoration relatively simple.

Following pages

Church's studio: clearly, the artist wanted to organize the space as an exchange and confrontation between occidental and oriental civilization. Church traveled constantly throughout his life, visiting South and Central America, Europe, Jamaica, Newfoundland, North Africa, and the Middle East, among other places. He kept detailed sketchbooks on these trips, with drawings and notes that he referred to upon his return to the studio. He later used these travel journals as inspiration for Olana.

Opposite
The main sitting room.

Left
El Khasne, Petra, Frederic Church, 1874. This large composition hangs above the mantel in one of the sitting rooms and reiterates the artist's fascination with oriental subjects. He wrote in his diary, "It is wonderful to see so lovely and luminous a color blazing out of the black stern frightful rocks, to behold the beautiful temple rich in sculptured ornament shining as if by its own internal light."

Below left
The Hudson mountains and the lower bell tower: Church chose this position high on a hill for Olana because of the romantic landscape he would view from his house. He had a particular attraction to this type of picturesque view, which was wild and reflected his ideal of nature.

"I have designed the house myself. It is Persian in style adapted to the climate and the requirements of modern life. The interior decorations and fittings are all in harmony with the external architecture. It stands at an elevation of 600 feet above the Hudson River and commands beautiful views of sky, mountains, rolling and savannah country, villages, forest and clearings. The noble River expands to a width of over two miles forming a lakelike sheet of water which is always dotted with steamers and other craft."
Frederic Church, 1877.

project. Not only did Church question each and every one of Vaux's drawings and proposals, but he also set about himself producing an impressive number of sketches and stencils. Church had made numerous sketches on his travels and now supplemented them by reading *Les Monuments modernes de la Perse* by Pascal Costes and *Les Arts arabes* by Jules Bogoin, which supplied him with most of his formal vocabulary.

The sham medieval fortress that was finally built was cuboid in structure with two large towers of unequal height, and a facade embellished by numerous Moorish-inspired details. While the lower part was stone, the upper part was of yellow, red, and black brick. Church's central idea had been to create a dwelling in which the domestic activities on the ground floor were organized entirely around a top-lit covered courtyard, but as his family continued to grow with the birth of two more children, Louis Palmer in 1870 and Isabel Charlotte in 1871, he was forced to relinquish this idea.

By 1871 the walls were built, and the following year the roof and ornamental details were finished. While his family moved into the second floor, Church embarked on the decoration of the ground floor, which was to take him no less than four years. The furnishings consisted of oriental objects and furniture and also baroque chairs handed down in his family, Shaker chairs, and furniture made to his own design. The overall effect was eclectic, as was characteristic of

the period, but Church contrived to create a surprisingly serene sense of equilibrium and harmony. His evocation of an oriental interior was tempered throughout by the use of simple forms and the judicious distribution of pieces of European origin. His own paintings, meanwhile, and his collection of works by other artists, lent each room its own distinctive character without lapsing into flamboyance.

In 1888, Church decided to build a new studio of substantial proportions, to comprise an observatory, a bedroom, and an enormous space for storage. The following year, he moved out of the New York studio that he had rented for thirty years. The new studio became, in turn, the object of long and painstaking reflection, which resulted in internal arrangements that were not far removed in style from those in the family dwelling.

Undeterred by all this building work, Church continued throughout with his alterations to the grounds at Olana, laying out paths, planting lines of trees to mask outbuildings, creating a vast lawn to the east over which visitors could enjoy distant views of the house, and to the south constructing a terrace with a views of the park below and the mountains beyond. To the west, meanwhile, the steeply sloping terrain revealed an altogether wilder landscape.

Church's health had by now started to give way. On April 7, 1900, he died in New York, having become too weak to return once more to Olana, the masterpiece over which he had labored for three decades.

ALPHONSE MUCHA

Arriving in Paris in 1887 to complete his studies, Alphonse Mucha (1860–1939) struggled in his early career, barely making a living doing illustrations for magazines and giving drawing lessons, until he was catapulted to fame by Sarah Bernhardt, who in 1894 commissioned him to design the poster for the Victor Sardou play *Gismonda*, in which she starred. The nearly life-size poster created a sensation with its strong composition, sensuous curves, decorative elements, and natural colors. Mucha became an overnight success and from then on the actress demanded he design not only the posters for her plays, but also all costumes and sets. This was the age of Mucha's enigmatic woman. Until the end of the First World War he worked almost exclusively in the applied arts, radically transforming the language of advertising and the arts of typography and book design. He also designed jewelry, overthrowing the conventional approach in order to stamp it with his inimitable art-nouveau style. He paid little attention to painting, however, until the day he conceived a grand design—inspired by a mixture of fierce nationalism (he was Czech by birth) and mysticism—to tell the story of the Slav people. This immense project, which he started in Paris around 1910, occupied him for the rest of his life. On his return to Czechoslovakia shortly after the country gained its independence, he went to live in the heart of Bohemia to complete his epic undertaking.

Right
An art-nouveau doorknocker. In 1902, Alphonse Mucha published his *Documents décoratifs*, an encyclopedia and sourcebook of the decorative arts. As well as a wealth of decorative motifs inspired by plants, flowers, animals, and the female form, it also illustrated decorative objects of all kinds, from furniture to dinner services and from lamps to jewelry of every description. Examples of Mucha's work in the decorative arts, less well known than his posters and illustrations, were added to these rooms after his death.

Right
An art-nouveau doorknocker. In 1902, Alphonse Mucha published his *Documents décoratifs*, an encyclopedia and sourcebook of the decorative arts. As well as a wealth of decorative motifs inspired by plants, flowers, animals, and the female form, it also illustrated decorative objects of all kinds, from furniture to dinner services and from lamps to jewelry of every description. Examples of Mucha's work in the decorative arts, less well known than his posters and illustrations, were added to these rooms after his death.

Far right
An oeil-de-boeuf window beside the main entrance.

Among Mucha's furniture in Prague

Opposite the castle in Prague stands a baroque palace (designed by an Italian architect) with two sculptures of giants brandishing their weapons over the doorway. Alphonse Mucha never lived in this handsome palace, yet everything here evokes his presence and reminds visitors that he was not merely an artist celebrated throughout the world, but also a Czech with a passionate attachment to his native culture. This building, which contains so many of his belongings, but where he never lived, seems to sum up his fate—for the last twenty years of his life, his immense, monumental, and interminable work exalting the history of the Slavs kept him away from the new Czech capital, which had commissioned it from him. Presented in 1928 as a gift to the city of Prague, this artistic folly has not been displayed in the city since 1939, when it was placed in storage to protect the paintings from the German occupation forces. A building designed especially to house the paintings designed by the architect Ladislas Saloun was never built, and the canvases were moved to the knights' hall of a remote and inaccessible Bohemian castle at Moravsky Krumlov where they have been exhibited as a complete cycle since 1967.

The origins of this project go back to 1908, when during a long visit to the United States Mucha attended a concert of music by Bedrich Smetana, a nationalist Bohemian composer, which inspired him with the idea of creating a cycle of paintings celebrating the civilization and tormented history of the Slav people. With funding provided by the American industrialist Charles Crane and his confidence bolstered by the advice of Ernest Denis, the Sorbonne historian of Bohemia, he embarked on a series of sketches for compositions measuring 30 x 24 feet. On his return to the newly independent Czechoslovakia in 1918, he set up a studio at Zbiroh, in part of an ancient castle put at his disposal. There he had some heavy and unwieldy scaffolding constructed on wheels so that he could move the paintings about, displaying two at a time, like opening pages of a gigantic book.

Mucha also had his living quarters within the castle. His son Jiri recalls this extraordinary arrangement, which to a child's eyes appeared almost unreal, "Living at Zbiroh suited him in every possible way. There was a long procession of enormous rooms with views over the countryside far below, stretching away to the horizon, which was blue, with forests the color of a painted bowl. Father moved in here with all the furniture and other items from his Paris studio, supplementing these with yet more antiques, draperies, and ornaments. The bedroom was furnished in Louis XVI style, with two beds arranged to impress beneath a canopy suspended from the ceiling. There was a drawing room, a dining room, a music room, a library, and, at the opposite end from these, the studio, reached by a passage above the side entrance to the castle. The castle's vaulted ceiling was constructed from small panes of glass . . . Inevitably there were leaks, and the floor was dotted everywhere with buckets. . . . there was also, precariously attached to the studio, a loggia with high, wide windows, jutting out over the cliff and a ravine."

This was the boy's first home, and doubtless the only one that he recognized as his own. And it was here that his father worked day and night, for weeks, months, and years on end, on his epic work. By 1912

Below and following pages

A compendium of innumerable different periods and styles, the dining room could not be further removed from the precepts espoused by the artist during his long residence in Paris. Then, along with most of the other pioneers of art nouveau, he argued in favor of a conceptual unity in interior design, even if this coherence was achieved by using contrasting influences. During his retreat to the depths of rural Bohemia, he mixed furniture and objects he had brought with him from his Paris residence on the rue du Val-de-Grâce with new acquisitions, without any undue concern for the overall effect. Photographs of his rooms in Paris reveal that he conformed to the extravagant eclecticism that prevailed at the turn of the century, while adding his own personal touches; the role of the mise-en-scène of his rooms was not merely to reflect his tastes and enthusiasms, but also to be a tangible monument to the extraordinary inventiveness and fertility of his artistic imagination.

"In his Paris studio he lived with his harmonium, his fireplace, his easels, his rolls of paper, and his medieval garments hanging from hooks. He used to design for the stage, and because of a sort of superstitious conservatism, always left the costumes, which he bought at the flea market, wherever the models happened to have dropped them. A helmet from the Thirty Years' War lay on the mantelpiece, a halberd was propped in the corner, and hanging from the easel was a black Moravian peasant's hat, embroidered with colored beads and trimmed with a long cock's feather."

Jiri Mucha, *Alphonse Maria Mucha,* Academy Editions, London, 1989.

62

Above
A table in the Mucha museum.

Left
A bust of the artist surrounded by a curious array of items. The decorative scheme of these rooms—the product of a temporary situation that persisted for many years, subsequently arranged by the fertile imagination of Mucha's writer son, Jiri, who returned to his country after the death of his father and the end of the Second World War—has an air of unreality, underlaid by a surrealist note struck by the accumulation of an eclectic mixture of objects of very diverse origins. Two life stories are expressed here in a manner that is unexpectedly complementary, creating bizarre, fairytale interiors that uncannily have survived the vicissitudes of Prague's twentieth-century intact.

Opposite
Rolls of Mucha drawings.

The large drawing room, hung with Mucha's work, is a strange art gallery, with no vanishing point nor any one point to which the eye is immediately drawn, and where everything conspires to create the sensation of drawing the visitor back into the past. Heady sensations and dizzying images combine to evoke distant memories. At first sight the decor is pure 1900, but more detailed scrutiny reveals that this spacious setting with its air of sensuality and melancholy is subverted by the intrusion of foreign elements such as Jiri Mucha's collections of African objects and stuffed birds.

"It was midnight, and there I was alone in my studio in the rue du Val-de-Grâce among my pictures, posters, and panels. I became very excited. I saw my work adorning the salons of the highest society or flattering people of the great world with smiling and ennobled portraits. I saw the books full of legendary scenes, floral garlands, and drawings glorifying the beauty and tenderness of women. This was what my time, my precious time, was being spent on, when my nation … was left to quench its thirst on ditch water. And in my spirit I saw myself sinfully misappropriating what belonged to my people. … it was midnight and, as I stood there looking at all these things, I swore a solemn promise that the remainder of my life would be filled exclusively with work for the nation."

Alphonse Mucha quoted in Derek Sayer, *The Coasts of Bohemia: A Czech History,* Princeton University Press, 1998.

"A crystal looking glass caught the weak shafts of light in its convoluted decoration, and the shaft of a bronze lamp rose from the ground like a plant that had given birth to an extravagantly large flower. Rows of paintings hung on the walls; but despite my best efforts, in the half-light I could make out only the general shapes, hazy colors, and a sense of mystery that rendered them all the more seductive."

Patrizia Runfola, *Le Palais de la mélancolie*, **Christian Bourgois, ed., Paris, 1994.**

he had completed only the first three canvases. This Herculean task—which he had originally imagined would take him four or five years—occupied nearly two decades. The first eleven paintings, ending with *Slavonic Liturgy*, were put on show at the Carolinum in 1919, to a favorable critical response although his style already seemed outmoded. Subsequently, they were successfully exhibited at the Brooklyn Museum.

In 1924 Mucha went to Mount Athos to learn more about Orthodox Christianity, a visit that strengthened his tendencies toward mysticism. Four years later he exhibited his monumental cycle in Prague, donating it to the city. Throughout all this, Mucha kept a small studio in Prague—which he used when he had to be away from Zbiroh—right in the heart of the city, beneath the dome of a bank building on the corner of Vodiakova Street and Wenceslas Square. There he painted small works, chiefly studies, and did a lot of drawing and photography using models, which he was unable to do in his remote Bohemian castle.

In 1925, Mucha decided to design his ideal villa in Prague, making a number of pen-and-ink sketches that give the disconcerting impression of a classical Ottoman building, with round roofs, broad and flat, curving in at the edges—a synthesis of Balkan and Turkish elements that owed nothing to the traditional architecture of Prague, nor even to the Secession or art nouveau.

Another design, more complete and in color, shows a large building with two curving wings punctuated with broad openings looking out over gardens. The imposing entrance is flanked by pillars and over-looked by a large circular balcony that also serves as a canopy; an imposing polychrome decorative feature tops the balcony. The remainder of the building is red and relatively sober in style. On the same axis as the entrance, stairs lead down to a round point surrounded by French-classical lawns. But it was all just a dream that never saw the light of day.

Today Mucha's apartments have been re-created in part in the handsome Kaunicky Palace in Prague. His son Jiri has been the devoted custodian for many years, while also leading a literary life of feverish activity. During the Second World War he joined his government in exile in London, and subsequently was condemned by Stalin's henchmen to four years of hard labor in the salt mines. Having served his sentence, he moved into this lovely palace, with its ground

floor and large atrium recalling a Venetian palazzo. He recounted the long history of the building to Patrizia Runfola, who first visited him before the "velvet revolution": "In medieval times . . . the building was a fortified castle with corner turrets, built in about the thirteenth century, when the dense forest that surrounded it was cleared in order to build residences for courtiers and high clergy on the rocky promontory. At that time the square looked very much as it does now, except that there was a deep moat separating the castle from the other dwellings. It must have been exceptionally beautiful. There was a chapel built and decorated by the most talented craftsmen available, who also decorated the cathedral of St. Guy. The same men are believed to have built the staircase and the great vaulted hall on the ground floor. According to some documents, the building was sold by Nicolas Nizohlad to Meynhardus Hergithift in 1363; whatever the case, in the late fourteenth or early fifteenth century the fortress became the property of the church. For a time it was occupied by the bishops of Litomûfiîce, followed by a cathedral canon by the name of Jan, a native of the village of Nepomuk. A distinguished lawyer, he played a prominent part in the political and religious debate that raged between the university and the crown. . . . The building's facade is visible from the Charles Bridge, and the walls, staircases, and rooms are all just as I found them."

When you cross the virtually deserted ground floor today to reach the immense drawing room on the first floor, it is like being in a bizarre museum, where the connoisseur who owns it also lives among his collections, allowing access only to close friends and distinguished visitors to the city. During the communist period, the most flamboyant characters would come to spend an evening here behind the closed velvet curtains, and artists, intellectuals, and nonconformists from the world over would come here to forget the iron hand of communism.

Jiri Mucha explained to Runfola what he had set out to achieve in this historic palace. "When I came to live here, I brought with me a lot of furniture and objects that had belonged to my father. I tried to re-create the atmosphere that was so characteristic of all his houses. The majority of these things came from his studio on rue du Val-de-Grâce in Paris, where he had lived for nearly fifteen years and which he had kept on. They have all traveled a lot—before coming to Bohemia he moved three times and made two return journeys from Paris to New

The harmonium from Alphonse Mucha's apartment. A surviving photograph from the early years of the twentieth century shows Paul Gauguin, who shared a studio with Mucha in Paris, playing Mucha's harmonium. Curiously, the photograph shows Gauguin wearing a jacket but no trousers. Mucha was a great lover of music who on several occasions collaborated with celebrated Czech musicians.

A poster by Alphonse Mucha, 1905, for the final American tour of *The Lady of the Camellias* starring Sarah Bernhardt in 1905–1906. It was to *"la divine Sarah"* that Mucha owed his fame and success after designing her poster for *Gismonda* in 1894. The poster brought him instant fame, and the great actress demanded that he design all her posters, costumes, and the sets for the plays in which she appeared over the next six years.

"I used to listen to his feelings about art, after his visit to the Tretyakov Gallery, where he had seen images that captured the essence of the Russian spirit, with its profoundly and proudly even-handed approach to everything, from mysticism to superstition, and with its tendency to use symbols, inherited from ancient Byzantine art: he maintained that for the Slavic peoples this was the only effective way of communicating their feelings."
Patrizia Runfola, *Le Palais de la mélancolie*, Christian Bourgois, ed., 1994.

York. He could have filled the whole building on his own. Later other things belonging to my mother's family were added, and I myself have contributed an ethnological collection of objects from Africa, South America, and the Pacific, which I have collected on my many travels." The result of all this is that somehow the story of one life has become wrapped up in the story of another, and that of the writer lies contained within that of his father, the great artist.

At the same time it is equally true that the overall effect of this extraordinary building—with its heavy velvet curtains, its red-upholstered armchairs, its costly oriental carpets, its astonishing accumulation of statuettes, including some by Auguste Rodin (to whom Mucha offered a warm welcome when he accompanied an exhibition of his work to Prague in 1902), and its wildly eclectic array of objects—is of a cabinet of curiosities. Here objects ancient and modern rub shoulders with the last artifacts of remote and lost worlds, and all in a setting of heady opulence redolent of the heyday of art nouveau. The few rays of light that filter into the room lend intense, profound, and intriguing life to these objects garnered (for their intellectual or aesthetic value rather than any monetary worth) from sumptuous pasts—the inviting furniture, with a plethora of deep divans; the round marble-topped table; the roll-top desk in precious wood; the Savonarola chair in dark wood; the precious carpets, thick and richly patterned; the bookcases with shelves weighed down by volumes printed in Czech, English, French, and German, encircling the room and yet not overwhelming it with their presence; the busts, masks, and bronze statuettes; the vases and carafes in Bohemian glass; the most incongruous collection of objects that would have delighted the Habsburg emperor Rudolf II; the gilded chandelier and the harmonium on which Gauguin played in the studio on rue Val-de-Grâce; and more, to the point where the eye becomes hopelessly confused among this mute concatenation of objects from beyond the grave. The walls are so densely lined with drawings and posters by Mucha that only the trompe-l'oeil barrel vaulting is easily distinguished. Among them all, one is particularly striking—a portrait of the first woman to serve in the Turkish government under Atatürk, the education minister Halide Edip Adivar. So coveted was this painting by the Turkish ambassador to Prague that every year he would go through the same ritual, paying a visit to Alphonse Mucha's son on the pretext of offering him his good

"Among all the many icons here, the Christ in polychrome wood hanging on the wall is a Romanesque work, almost certainly from Brittany. It appears in many of the photos of my father's Paris studio in rue du Val-de-Grâce. . . . I knew that, ever since his childhood spent in the religious foundation at Brno in Moravia, Alphonse Mucha liked to surrounded himself with religious artifacts."

Jiri Mucha, quoted in *Le Palais de la mélancolie*, Christian Bourgois, ed., 1994.

wishes, and all the while hoping that this time he would offer it as a gift to the Turkish government.

A muffled hush reigns in these cloistered spaces, with their baroque and eclectic atmosphere, and in the drawing room especially, more *fin-de-siècle* Parisian in spirit than Czech. This is a place of memories, but untainted by either sadness or regret. And perhaps one day *The Apotheosis of Slav Nations* will be on view again in Prague, together with the other colossal paintings in the epic cycle that Alphonse Mucha hoped to dedicate to world peace.

For Mucha, the winter of 1938–1939 was a period of acute nostalgia. Still living in the temporary quarters that had been his home for twenty years, he was overwhelmed at the prospect of the end of everything—his life, his immense artistic dream, and his country. "Summer is gone, autumn is over, and when will this winter ever end? Little by little I am losing hope. And my health—how I count on it! How precious my time has been. Every single minute, dear and precious—and now I squander months at a time. My work will survive—but the strength of youth? My work will not disappear. No—for as long as I live it will tear ever deeper into my soul. But what matters most is the subject matter that informs the work—and the time is come! When it disappears, everything will disappear. It will all be over. Now both my passion and my time hang in shreds, and there are no pleasures left to me."

"Everything in this house had a long history … The four-poster bed in which I slip into the arms of Morpheus each night comes from the Waldstein family … and belonged to the famous captain who inspired Schiller's great drama. Subsequently, the destiny of objects being so much longer and more mysterious than our own, it was lost in the mists of time and crossed the Atlantic. In the early twentieth century it reemerged in the house of Emmy Destinn, a famous opera singer who sang with Caruso in New York. Sold after her death, it was once more lost to view. Finally it appeared in the window of a Prague antique shop, the owner of which offered it without success to my father. There it stayed for several years, until after the war, when I bought it in exchange for a small painting, a portrait of a woman painted in Paris. Many years later, by which time the antiquary was dead, his son asked me if I knew anyone who would be interested in buying the painting. So I bought the painting through a friend and that's how I managed to have them both."
Jiri Mucha in *Le Palais de la mélancolie*, Patrizia Runfola, Christian Bourgois, ed., Paris, 1994.

RENÉ
MAGRITTE

The darling of the French surrealist movement, René Magritte (1898–1967) left his native Belgium for Paris in 1927. There he painted the first of his alphabet paintings, combining words and images, and his work was reproduced in *La Révolution surréaliste*. But by the end of 1929 his honeymoon period with André Breton and his circle had come to an end, and Magritte returned to Brussels. He moved to the suburbs at Jette, where his modest home soon became a battleground for the latent conflict simmering between the artist and his wife, Georgette—while he designed post-cubist bedroom furniture, she was busy decorating the living room in the most conventional petit-bourgeois style. The flagrant contrast between their two approaches to decoration, with the piquant addition of Magritte's paintings on the walls, combined to produce an effect that was frankly bizarre. It was in these uncommon surroundings that the select coterie of Belgian surrealists, unwilling to submit to the dictates of their French colleagues, used to meet at frequent intervals. Louis Scutenaire (who in 1942 set down a scrupulously detailed description of the house as though it were a museum), E.L.T. Mesens, Paul Nougé, Marcel Lecomte, Paul Colinet, and the composer André Souris were among the regular attendees of these meetings, where both poetry and music were performed. It was in the dining room here that Magritte chose to work, never using the studio that he and his brother shared on the other side of the courtyard, from which they launched their admittedly unsuccessful careers in advertising.

Part of the artist's work consists of pastiches of paintings and drawings from the past. The metamorphosis of the most mundane scenes of domestic life and the placing of familiar objects in a void form one of the most striking aspects of his art as seen here in *In Memoriam Mack Sennett*, (1934). In addition, he enjoyed playing on the relationship between an object and the word that signified it. *The Treachery of Images* (Ceci n'est pas une pipe) is perhaps the most famous example of this paradoxical approach, along with *The Key of Dreams* (La Clef des songes, 1930) in which an egg is labeled an acacia and a woman's shoe as the moon. In 1948 he developed his *Alphabet des révélations*, in which black silhouettes of animals and objects take on a symbolic significance that is entirely up to the viewer's interpretation.

"The banality common to all things, that is the mystery."
René Magritte, *La Fée ignorée.*

The dreamlike daily life of René Magritte

In the summer of 1930, after spending nearly three years in a small villa at Le Perreux-en-Marne in order to be closer to the "Vatican," or the surrealist circle ruled with a rod of steel by André Breton, René Magritte and his wife, Georgette, left Paris to return to Brussels. In Paris Magritte had met Miró, Dalí, and Max Ernst. Eventually, after many failed attempts, he was received into the inner sanctum, where he met Paul Eluard and Breton himself. But in December 1929 an incident at Breton's studio caused a clash of wills between the two men that was to have major repercussions as Magritte was expelled from the circle. Left without their support in a time of economic hardship when galleries and collectors were going bankrupt, Magritte had no choice but to return to Belgium.

He and Georgette moved into a house at 135 rue Esseghem in the Brussels suburb of Jette, a quiet and bland middle-class district. As observed dryly by their friend Goesmans, "He was fond of this district peopled by gas tanks, and he remained loyal to it through thick and thin. There was no telephone at this point." The other side of the street had not yet been built, and from his window Magritte looked out over fields, greenhouses, and market gardens as well as monuments of the industrial era.

The building is an example of the small houses typical of the suburbs of Brussels, a mere twenty feet wide, with a red-tiled roof, a red-brick facade, white-stone lintels, and a balcony on the second floor. The Magrittes occupied the ground floor, reaching their apartment by a narrow corridor that led to the staircase, in which, as described by Jan Ceuleers, the architect had indulged in one single flight of fancy, "This dark space was lightened by means of a design in muddy stone, painted and decorated with a frieze of shells also in a sandy color, above reddish-brown paneling, more suited to a monument wishing to be seen as historic." Magritte's inexplicable fondness for this anodyne suburb is evident in a number of his paintings, including *The Empire of Light* (1952).

Magritte's apartment was extremely modest. The living room, which looked out on to the street, was furnished with a small marble-topped occasional table, two chairs (later replaced by a pair of capacious armchairs), a divan, a small glass-fronted bookcase reserved for the best books, a chest of drawers, an upright piano, a lectern, and a chandelier, initially made of hemp and later of crystal. The wallpaper, with an oriental pattern in blue, was later painted over, also in blue. The artist's favorite paintings (done by his own hand), which he had decided to keep, were hung here. The absurd side to all this did not escape his friend and biographer Louis Scutenaire, who described the room as being "graciously furnished in an eighteenth-century style enlivened by a large black piano with white teeth, a modern upright piano." The wide sash window, framed by heavy brown curtains, appeared in one of Magritte's most famous paintings, *The Human Condition* (1933), in which a tranquil rural landscape, half-real and half-imaginary, overlaps onto a canvas placed on an easel.

"I did paintings in which I depicted objects looking as they do in the real world, in a way that was objective enough to be upsetting; they show themselves capable of provoking beauty in a certain way that becomes part of the real world from which the objects were borrowed, thus creating a perfectly natural exchange of places."

René Magritte, *La Ligne de vie II, L'Invention collective no. 2*, Brussels, February 1940.

Above
The front doorbell.

Right
Magritte's easel in the little dining room where he painted wearing his suit and slippers.

The cramped dining room that doubled as Magritte's studio; all his materials had to be cleared away at mealtimes.

"Painters are painters, that is to say that for them thinking of an object can be reduced to the exploitation of that object for the benefit of their painting. 'That gesture would be good,' they say, 'that scene, that tree, that color.' And that is enough to limit their thoughts ineluctably to the play of appearances, to bar them from any type of true effectiveness. *Ceci n'est pas une pipe,* counters Magritte, quite rightly. . . . Understanding the world by transforming it, that is without any doubt our true function. To think of an object is to change it."

Paul Nougé, *Les Images défendues.*

Left
The austere bathroom, which brings to mind the settings for many of the artist's paintings. For Magritte, ideas "cannot be seen through the eyes. Ideas have no visual appearance, so no image can represent an idea." Through this type of syllogism, he attempted to explain how his philosophy of resemblances was a sort of paradox, since the most insignificant of objects had the possibility of becoming the most enigmatic and therefore the most fascinating. "Resemblance emerges as the essential element of the act of thinking. Thought resembles by becoming that which the world offers it and in restoring what is offered to it to the mystery without which neither the world nor thought could have any possibility of existence. Inspiration is the event from which resemblance arises. Thought resembles only through being inspired," (catalogue to the Liège exhibition, 1960). The sparseness and simplicity of Magritte's everyday existence were a response to this demand, which precluded the outward and redundant symbols of the surrealism of André Breton's circle.

Above
A play of perspectives.

Opposite
Everyday objects.

"The art of painting, as I see it, is a means of making poetic images visible. They show riches and details that our eyes recognize with ease: trees, skies, stones, objects, people, etc. They also have a meaning that we can grasp with our intellect, if only we can let go of our fanatical need to give meaning to things in order to make use of them or to master them."
René Magritte, 'L'Art poétique, 'La Carte d'après nature, January 1955.

The classic mantelpiece arrangement, meanwhile, featuring a pair of candelabra and a clock, all surmounted by a mirror, is to be found in *Time Transfixed* (1938–9), in which a black railroad engine comes steaming out of the wall.

This was the room where Magritte received his friends, where they wrote their *Correspondances* tracts, and where André Souris composed his music. Magritte loved music; his favorite composers, according to Scutenaire, included "Brahms, Bach, Ravel, Lalo, Duparc, Churchill, Sibelius, Fauré, Debussy, Satie, Chopin, Smetana, and a hundred others." This passion soon made its appearance in his work, in the form of the thirty or so collages he produced between 1925 and 1927 using sheet music. In another example, *The Menaced Assassin* (1927), a sort of tableau vivant inserted in a conventional setting, shows a man in a suit listening to a gramophone, while a naked woman lies on a red velvet divan and a number of enigmatic figures look on, or wait in the adjoining room. Magritte owned just such a gramophone, and often listened to it while he painted. Also, an unwieldy double-bass appears in *The Happy House* (1953), while in *The Central Story* (1928) a trombone stands next to a suitcase.

Like the living room, the bedroom, reached through double doors, gives tangible form to the sharp difference of opinion between René and Georgette in matters of decoration. The wardrobe and linen chest, designed by the artist in a cubist vein, are painted with red lacquer, while the stools and screen are painted black. By contrast, the large bed opposite the fireplace is reminiscent of Pompadour style, and this, with a sprinkling of Georgette's ornaments, successfully shatters the stylish unity sought by Magritte, who designed this ensemble for his marriage in 1922. '"The atmosphere of the greenish-blue bedroom with its accents of red and black," notes Scutenaire, "is reminiscent of some of his well-known paintings." *In Memoriam Mack Sennett* (1936) shows the open door of a wardrobe revealing a nightgown still molded to the form of a woman's body. The room also appears in a dreamlike vision in *Personal Values* (1952), where sky and clouds replace the walls; an enormous comb lies on the bed; an equally enormous badger perches on top of the wardrobe, and a green glass stands beside an oversized pencil and a strange pouf on one of the two rugs beneath a ceiling covered in flaking gray paint.

The kitchen, which was virtually part of the dining room, would be unremarkable were it not for the important part it played in Magritte's life. Scutenaire explains, "The dining room was where Magritte painted, ate his meals, received visitors, and lived his daily life. It offered a view of the aviary filled with birds until the birds flew away, when their former home was used as firewood." It was in this small room, with its pale pink walls above a gray skirting board, and its rustic Breton-style table with a matching pair of chairs and armchairs, that he painted most of his paintings from this lengthy period of his life.

Magritte was quite happy to work with very few materials, as noted by Scutenaire, ". . . an easel, a box of paints, a palette, twelve brushes, one or two sheets of white paper in a box, an eraser, a stump, a pair of dressmakers' scissors, a stub of charcoal, and an old black pencil." But it all had to be carefully put away before meals, "The frugal nature of this arrangement . . . was not without its inconveniences for the artist. As the room was of modest dimensions, he would get tied up in knots, hemmed in as he was on all sides by the table, the door, and the stove. He would bang himself on one and burn himself on the other, and every time the door opened with all the comings and goings, it would knock his arm and his brush would veer off course. The sun would beat in through the high window, bringing him to a sweat and falling directly onto the canvas, transforming it into a mirror casting dazzling reflections. On dull days and after sunset, meanwhile, he could hardly see as the light was so awkwardly distributed." He never wanted a proper studio and always worked in a suit, so deeply did he loathe all the outward trappings of the artist's life. "Magritte was a nonconformist through and through," confirms Roisin, "even in the artistic world. So when it came to clothes, they were all in hats, cravats, and beards, while René wore a suit. . . . The company he sought out most was that of literary hacks." He undoubtedly identified with his famous archetypal figure, dressed in a black overcoat and bowler hat, who appears in numerous paintings including *The Masterpiece or Mysteries of the Horizon* (1955).

In his work, familiar, ordinary objects became unfamiliar and extraordinary, "We know only things that can or cannot be used." Kitchen items appeared in a number of his works, for instance the piece of cheese under a glass cover in *This is a Piece of Cheese* (1935–6), and the baguettes flying in close formation in *The Golden Legend* (1958). Paul Nougé describes the process at work here, "Yet here are all the familiar objects . . . all the appointed participants in our lives, but evoked in such

The parlor, with the piano and the conventional bourgeois furniture chosen by Mme. Magritte—a taste the artist did not share. The pair of black china dogs speaks volumes about Georgette's concept of decoration. But in its blatant opposition between Magritte's aesthetic and his wife's conformist aspirations, this room is already a fragment of his universe; the discrepancy created in this way between his painting and a typically bourgeois way of life contains the germ of a surrealistic image with its own humor.

On the wall hangs Magritte's 1947 painting *Olympia*. In the 1940s, Magritte painted a number of female nudes of almost photographic verisimilitude combined with rocks of extravagant form or simply set in front of a coastal scene or in a forest clearing, so creating a sense of unreality and a queasy, out-of-kilter eroticism.

"The aim of the art of painting is to perfect they way we see things by means of a purely visual perception of the external world using only the sense of sight. A painting created with this goal in mind is a way of replacing natural spectacles that are always the same or always predictable."
René Magritte, *F. A. no. 18*, March 1969, quoted in *Ecrits complets*, collected and edited by André Blavier, *Tout l'art*, Flammarion 2001.

Above
A lamp in the living room, typical of Georgette's taste.

Right
Magritte's telephone: curiously, Magritte made very little use of modern objects in his iconography. While his male figures wear contemporary dress, the objects that surround them are relatively timeless. On the whole, Magritte's repertoire belonged more to the cubists of the preceding generation than to the surrealism of Paris. He seems to have preferred to preserve intact the world of his childhood memories, and also that of his dreams, which frequently harked back to the previous century, as in *Souvenir of a Journey* (1955).

Below

The bedroom, with the wardrobe designed by Magritte and the bed chosen by Georgette.

Right

Time Transfixed, René Magritte, 1938–9. The steam engine chugging out of the fireplace at full speed is probably a reference to an 1895 railway accident at the Montparnasse train station, when a train ploughed through the station wall and the engine was left hanging in thin air above the square below. This extraordinary event caught the public imagination, and a commemorative postcard was published. Magritte was greatly preoccupied with the striking or startling aspect of the work of art, believing that the perfect painting "produces an intense effect for only a very short time, and feelings resembling the initial feeling are tainted by habit . . . In accordance with this law, the viewer should be open to experiencing a unique moment of awareness and admit his powerlessness in prolonging it."

Below
Objects from the familiar and dreamlike world of Magritte
in the room under the eaves, a number of which may be
found in his paintings. Already during the war and again in
the 1960s, Magritte produced gouaches and collages in
which musical scores played an important part, contributing
to a poetic atmosphere that was removed from the effects
he usually sought in his paintings. Even when they use
familiar images such as pipes, bowling pins, and flying birds
these works on paper are frequently dismissed by
specialists. Most of these works are considered of minor
importance in his oeuvre; this betrays a complete lack of
awareness of Magritte's attachment to music.

a way that when we return to the world, that which was familiar to the
point of invisibility suddenly acquires a remarkable and charming
solidity that calls into question its future relationship with us. The
universe has changed; nothing is ordinary any more."

Cramped though it was, the dining room, like the entrance hall, had
a bookcase, containing volumes of the horror stories that Magritte so
enjoyed. He loved books, and his paintings reflect a playful and
disconcerting relationship between objects and words, as in *The
Treachery of Images* (Ceci n'est pas une pipe, 1929) but they also suggest
the capacity of literature to amaze, as in *The Submissive Reader* (1928). In
a canvas entitled *Reproduction Forbidden* (1927), which depicts a man
standing in front of a mirror that offers him no reflection but instead
reproduces what the viewer sees of him, a book by Edgar Allen Poe is
placed on a marble console. The hall also contains a hat stand on which
are hung the overcoat, the bowler hat, and the umbrella that play such
prominent parts in the artist's world, as in the two versions of his
painting entitled *Hegel's Holiday* (1958 and 1959).

The Magritte family lived in Jette for twenty-four years, and the
artist spent the last ten years of his life in the Schaerbeek district. This
urban world, so typical of working-class Brussels, appears in *La
Poitrine* (1961), in which little houses are squashed together in cheerful
confusion to form a hill in the shape of a breast.

Right

The studio, on the other side of the small internal courtyard, where Magritte never painted, but where he worked with his brother as a graphic designer in advertising. Magritte's advertising work gave him the opportunity to display his remarkable talents in this field, although he was always careful to distinguish between his pure art and any work undertaken for commercial gain. The brothers' relative lack of success in this area may also have encouraged Magritte to give it little prominence. But it certainly provided him with a testing ground where he developed not only his own imagery but also, and above all, a conception of the nature of the image that remains unusual to this day.

Below

In the studio a wistful putto stands in front of the drawing board where Magritte worked on numerous posters.

ROSA BONHEUR

Opposite
Paying scant attention to the social conventions of the time, Rosa Bonheur always preferred to dress eccentrically, and even obtained special permission from the Préfecture de police to wear her own interpretation of men's clothing. When working in her studio, as shown in her *Self-Portrait*, she wore an outfit of her own invention that married her idiosyncratic tastes with practical considerations and the codes of propriety in force in France in the second half of the nineteenth century.

Above
The Château de By and the studio that Bonheur created in the heart of the forest of Fontainebleau. The work that she had carried out to enlarge this small *manoir* at Thomery included the erection of the studio and numerous garden buildings, including a menagerie. Thus she created a world that rotated around her passion for the animal kingdom and her own conception of nature.

Top right
Rosa Bonheur.

Rosa Bonheur (1822–1899) was from an artistic background; her father was a minor (but reasonably talented) landscape painter who encouraged his talented daughter to spend time copying paintings at the Louvre. At nineteen years of age she had the good fortune to have two works accepted at the Salon of 1841, where they attracted favorable attention. At subsequent Salons she enjoyed her greatest successes and become recognized as the foremost "animalier" or animal painter. As early as 1845 she was awarded a bronze medal, and in 1848 she received the highest accolade, a gold medal, and received her first official commission. Collectors of her work—of whom there were to be many—included the duc de Morny and the wife of Napoleon III, Empress Eugénie. At the end of the year 1860, she left her Paris studio for the Château de By at Thomery, near Fontainebleau, which she had bought the previous year. She restored the buildings, and installed an immense studio and a menagerie of wild animals, while every type of domestic animal gamboled in the grounds. She lived there with her partner Nathalie Micas, and later with the American Anna Klumpke, her pupil and biographer. At By she spent the last years of her long life, which had been distinguished by continuing and undiminished success, not only in France but also in Britain and America, where a veritable cult grew up around her work.

" 'As for the organizing of my palette, first I put the greens, the blues, next white, then the yellows, the reds, the browns, and finally the blacks. Here they are, just as I said.' Rosa Bonheur picked up one of her palettes. 'Emerald green, Veronese green, cobalt green, chrome-oxide green, cobalt blue, ultramarine, Prussian blue; silver white; Naples yellow, yellow ocher, gold ocher, burnt gold ocher, raw and burnt sienna; vermilion no. 1, Venetian red, Indian red, Van Dyck red, red ocher, burnt lake, madder lake, Van Dyck brown; ivory black, peach black.' "

Rosa Bonheur, quoted in *Rosa Bonheur, sa vie, son oeuvre*, Anna Klumpke, Flammarion, 1908.

Rosa Bonheur's Noah's Ark in the Forest of Fontainebleau

In 1859 Rosa Bonheur bought the Château de By at Thomery, near Fontainebleau. The earliest part of the building dated from the early fifteenth century, when it was the modest dwelling of the royal beekeeper. A century later it passed to Henri de Bye, commander of Saint-Jean-de-Latran, and his descendants lived there for almost four hundred years. By the time Bonheur bought it the structure was in need of major repairs, and as part of these renovations she installed her studio in a picturesque brick wing of the building. She also lost no time in populating the extensive grounds with a menagerie of animals including sheep, oxen, *moufflons* (wild mountain sheep), horses, and even lions.

By this time she was already an artist of renown, and by the end of her life she had become the first woman to be awarded the Légion d'honneur, which the Empress Eugénie presented as she proclaimed, "genius has no sex." Born in Bordeaux in 1822, the daughter of a minor landscape painter and follower of Saint-Simon, Bonheur enjoyed a meteoric start to her career. At the age of nineteen she sent two canvases, *Chèvres et Moutons (Goats and Sheep)* and *Lapins (Rabbits Nibbling Carrots)*, to the jury of the Salon and was admitted with ease. Subsequently she exhibited at the Salon every year until 1848, when she was awarded the gold medal and received a commission from the provisional government of the Second Republic for a large composition entitled *Ploughing in the Nivernais.* And on top of all this, she was appointed director of the Ecole d'Art pour Jeunes Filles on rue Touraine-Saint-Germain in Paris, a position her father held before her.

The Second Empire brought her fresh triumphs. The duc de Morny, interior minister and half-brother of the emperor, commissioned a painting from her and bought another in his private capacity; her *Grain Market* won her another gold medal at the Salon of 1855; and in 1867 she exhibited at the Exposition universelle in Paris, where Empress Eugénie bought *Sheep by the Sea.* In 1889 Bonheur saw Buffalo Bill Cody's Wild West Show at the Paris Exposition and made sketches for a portrait, *The Buffalo Hunt,* which became the basis for Cody's publicity campaign. She was later received at Fontainebleau by Napoleon III, and in 1898 was honored with a visit at her château by Queen Isabella of Spain.

Although some critics accused her of being a self-appointed ambassador for the English school of painting, and a few caricatured

Above
A cupboard holding the artist's tools and books.

her as the *"Bouguereau des vaches,"* lampooning her as the animal world's equivalent of the derided master of ultrarealistic nudes, her success continued unabated until her death in 1899. Feted in England and admired in America, which she visited in 1893, she was a formidable figure whose alternative lifestyle did nothing to detract from her popularity. Bonheur lived, first, with her childhood friend Nathalie Micas, and after Nathalie's death in 1889 with an American painter, Anna Klumpke, who later became her biographer. Also, in 1857 Bonheur received special police authorization, ostensibly for "reasons of health" to wear men's clothing in public, with restrictions against appearing thus at "spectacles, balls, or other public meeting places." The permit was renewable every six months.

Her studio, which she had enlarged in 1895 in order to accommodate vast canvases such as the one destined for the Exposition universelle of 1900, remains more or less as it is shown in an engraving of the visit of Empress Eugénie accompanied by a cohort of ladies in crinolines. The imposing fireplace, flanked by a pair of sculptures of seated dogs by her brother Auguste, is topped by a mounted skull with an impressive pair of antlers. But what the engraving does not show is the host of stuffed birds and other hunting trophies, and the unbelievable state of chaos that reigned in a world devoted exclusively to the artist's obsession with animals. She also installed a small study containing a desk where she wrote letters or consulted her wealth of reference material, and a small salon or boudoir. Her studio was thus an independent apartment, carefully furnished according to contemporary tastes, with no discernible preference for any particular style. Although she kept a studio in Paris, first in rue de l'Ouest and from late 1853 in rue d'Assas, the Château de By meant total freedom, far removed from the social whirl and—as far as was possible—from all but the barest human presence.

A fervent patriot, when Bonheur learned of the Prussian advance on Paris in 1870 she organized the defense of her estate—though she roundly refused to countenance the slaughter of her beloved animals to feed the starving city. Although relatively conformist in her views (she was by no means indifferent to honors and awards), Bonheur was a rebel spirit, with dubious morals for the period, who was never happier than when she was close to nature. The horseback trek that she and Nathalie Micas made through the Pyrenees in the summer of 1850 was certainly one of her most cherished memories. Every time she discovered a new wilderness she was smitten; she found a tour of the Highlands of Scotland in 1856 hugely inspiring, and her visit to America kindled an abiding fascination with the native American peoples and a passion for the animals that roamed the great plains at will. She devoted her last years to re-creating her impressions of the American West—still wild at that time—and her studio contains a large sketch showing magnificent horses galloping across an apparently infinite prairie.

"I try to follow the example of Schiller. He said that what we give to art should come from inside us, and what we take from the outside world should be reborn within us. If we ignore the divine inspiration that must give birth to every painting, we will feel nothing and the work will remain lifeless."

Rosa Bonheur, quoted in *Rosa Bonheur, sa vie, son oeuvre*, Anna Klumpke, Flammarion, 1908.

Preceding pages
The studio, showing the pair of dogs sculpted by her brother, the plethora of hunting trophies and stuffed animals, and one of Bonheur's last paintings.

Below
Shepherd of the Pyrenees, Rosa Bonheur, 1888. After the death of her father, Bonheur went on a journey with Nathalie Micas through the Pyrenees, where she made sketches and preparatory drawings for numerous paintings, including this one.

Opposite
The artist's comprehensive archives, with plaster casts.

In order to fully recapture in paint the impressions and emotions she experienced on her travels within France and abroad, Bonheur required peace and privacy. Although she could be outspoken, deployed considerable self-assurance and a will of iron, and enjoyed being positively brazen and provocative, she was nevertheless a deeply private and controlled person. Only the women with whom she shared her life were able to elicit any confidences, and even these were carefully edited, being limited to her family history, of which she felt proud, and to her artistic tastes, which were primarily infatuations with particular subjects rather than with any particular genre of painting. A realist by definition, she took her inspiration chiefly from the minor Dutch masters and from English animal painters of the eighteenth and early nineteenth centuries. It became commonplace, indeed, to view her as a rival to Charles Landseer, court painter to Queen Victoria.

A clue to the character of the mistress of By may be found in an article by Emile Cantrel that appeared in *L'Artiste* in 1859, in which he compared her to George Sand, "There is a very close relationship between these two talents—Mlle Rosa Bonheur frequently reads George Sand, who is her favorite author, and I should not be at all surprised if Mme Sand does not feel a similar admiration for the landscapes of Rosa Bonheur. George Sand has a special genius for describing landscapes, and in her paintings Rosa Bonheur makes the trees sing and gives eloquent voice to the animals, the grass, and the clouds. Both are able to understand the mute symphonies of the universe and to express them in the harmonious language of art ..."

GUSTAVE MOREAU

Opposite
The magnificent staircase linking Gustave Moreau's two studios.

Above
In this handsome house on rue de La Rochefoucauld in Paris, Moreau created an original body of work that stood on the fringes of the symbolist movement spreading throughout Europe. At the end of his life he transformed the house into a sort of mausoleum, where visitors would be able to follow the major stages in his development and view his drawings and paintings in their entirety. The monumental facade was added to the building in 1895, with a view to transforming it from a private house into a museum.

Top right
Gustave Moreau.

Gustave Moreau (1826–1898) came from a cultivated background; his father, Louis, was a well-known architect. His parents were liberal-minded enough to encourage him in his declared ambition to be an artist, which as his mother recalled was clear early, "from the age of eight [he] was constantly drawing everything he saw." He enrolled in the Ecole des Beaux-Arts in Paris, where he failed to be selected for the Prix de Rome. Undeterred, he organized his own protracted trip to Italy, from 1857 to 1859. In 1864 he submitted *Oedipus and the Sphinx* to the Salon, which received it favorably. Five years later he exhibited *Jupiter and Europa* and *Prometheus*, which earned him not only a medal but also some harsh criticism, as a result of which he did not exhibit at the Salon again until 1876. He also refused a number of public commissions, but accepted membership in the illustrious Institut de France. In his lifetime he held only one one-man show, at the Galerie Goupil in 1886. In 1892 he became a professor at the Ecole des Beaux-Arts in Paris, where he was hugely popular with his students, including Matisse and Rouault. As collectors of his work were few, from 1862 he began planning to turn his house into a *musée sentimental* containing the bulk of his work. This projected was completed in 1895, shortly before his death.

Moreau's rich collection of faience displayed on the ornate credenza. When Moreau drew his last breath, on April 18, 1872, at the age of seventy-two, his death passed virtually unnoticed, with only a simple funeral mass at the neighboring Church of the Trinity followed by a modest burial in the cemetery of Montparnasse. He had given instructions to his heir, Henri Rupp, to destroy his personal correspondence and not to circulate his portrait. Right up to the very end of his life Moreau worked tirelessly to create a sort of domestic shrine devoted to the shades of those who had shared his life, and the museum was to be organized around these memories. He was also determined at all costs to put the finishing touches on this curious bequest to the nation. Even as he lay on his deathbed, he elicited the faithful Rupp's assistance in this task, "Stretched out on his bed of pain, wracked by excruciating agonies, he was still obsessed by his customary concerns. He had his latest sketch brought in—on his instructions I would alter a detail, change a tone, tone down a too-bright flash of white."

The coded museum of Gustave Moreau

In his novel *Monsieur de Phocas,* Jean Lorrain imagined the vicissitudes of an aristocratic young man unfortunate enough to fall under the spell of a painter he encountered. The artist commands him to go to the Musée Gustave Moreau and there surrender to "the atmosphere of massacre and murder" that reigns in this place of corpses and bloodshed. Then, impregnated with the "stench of blood," he will find the strength to slay his tormentor and persecutor. Moreau's works offered inspiration to numerous writers of his day, including Joris-Karl Huysmans, Maurice Barrès, Le Sâr Peladan, Elémir Bourges and Léon Bloy, and in subsequent years he proved equally fascinating to André Breton, Georges Bataille and many others. "My discovery of the Musée Gustave Moreau when I was sixteen," confessed Breton, "has conditioned my attitude to love ever since. Beauty, love—it was here that they were first revealed to me, through a thousand faces, a few women's poses." And he concludes, "I was utterly bewitched." Moreau's friend Edgar Degas, by contrast, felt a vague unease when he paid a visit to the house during its conversion into this unusual museum.

It is impossible to enter this strange sanctuary of some twelve hundred paintings and watercolors and nearly thirteen thousand drawings without falling prey to a slightly queasy sensation, a cocktail of anxiety and vertigo. The sheer number of paintings in their gilded frames and the paneled walls—the scenes inspired mostly by the Bible and classical mythology—all conspire to strengthen the overarching impression of an ethereal but tragic wonderment where beauty flirts dizzyingly with violent death. Théophile Gautier's verdict, "His painting, so bizarre and willfully eccentric, is designed for the sensitive, the exquisite, and the curious," would still hold true today, were it not for the fact that the scale and value of Moreau's aesthetic enterprise have since been accorded their due recognition.

Moreau conceived the idea for this museum when his father died in 1862, but he started to put it into effect only after another bereavement, the death of his companion Alexandrine Dureux in 1890. The pain of this loss exacerbated his already melancholy disposition. His old friend Henri Rupp recalled that he "descended into that state of overwhelming grief that follows irreversible tragedies," adding that, "More than ever, he sought refuge in his work—it became his consolation." He still possessed virtually his entire oeuvre, having sold only a very few works to the handful of collectors who were interested in buying it. He remained undecided, however, about the form that he should give to this museum that had been his obsession for so many years. Should he turn the house into an idiosyncratic museum in its own right, and display his paintings and drawing somewhere else altogether? Should he give all his work to the nation,

Moreau's bedroom, which he transformed into a shrine, was not originally intended to be open to the public, though the room in which he died was arranged with meticulous care. Portraits of friends (including Edgar Degas) and relatives surrounded his bed. Watercolors by Chassériau, Fromentin, and Berchère and a fine drawing by Nicolas Poussin lined the narrow passageway leading to the room. In an adjacent room, Moreau installed a small boudoir in memory of his companion, Alexandrine.

Below
The chessboard at the foot of the bed.

Opposite
Vases from Moreau's collection.

"I think about my death and the fate of my poor little works, of all these compositions that I am at such pains to reunite, since separately they will perish, but taken together they convey some small idea of the kind of artist I was and of the surroundings in which I liked to dream."
Gustave Moreau, note written on the study for *Delilah at her Toilet*, Christmas 1862.

in one huge donation? In the end, he decided to turn his house into a museum that would document both his life and his art. He hoped it would reveal the development of his work in intimate detail, and that it would allow the public to study his most ambitious pieces closely. With this end in mind, he had no reservations about producing modified copies of works that he had sold and new versions of ones with which he was not completely satisfied.

In 1895, he engaged the architect Albert Lafon to carry out a complete refurbishment of the immense building at 14 rue de la Rochefoucauld in the district of Nouvelle Athènes, where he had lived since 1852. The instructions he gave to Lafon were meticulous, as he had already planned the entire hanging scheme in his head according to his own metaphorical program. He completely transformed the second and third stories into two softly lit galleries, reached from the first floor by an unusual spiral staircase. In one of the galleries he hung his most imposing works, including *The Suitors*, *The Daughters of Thespius*, *Hesiod and the Muses*, *Chimaeras*, and *The Mystical Flower*. The other contained two self-portraits and compositions including *Jupiter and Semele* and *The Life of Humanity*, as well as Moreau's superb revolving display system for his watercolors, wash drawings, and pastels.

His private quarters, meanwhile, were remodeled to become a small and private museum. His former bedroom gave place to a small boudoir that he filled with the belongings of his faithful companion Alexandrine. In 1890 he bought back all the mementoes that told the story of a secret liaison that had lasted twenty-five years in order to erect this shrine to his memory. The bedroom was given over largely to items from his mother's bedroom, including most notably her fine Empire bed. The wine-colored walls in the dining room set off celebrated works such as *Orpheus*, *The Chimaera*, *Sappho*, and *Young Man and Death*, housed a credenza with a display of Italian faience of

Right
Moreau devoted fastidious attention to the arrangement of the small drawing room, or study, as he did with every other room in the house. Through a highly sophisticated network of interrelationships, Moreau intended the items on display in the house to narrate the development of his inner life. All this was therefore to be preserved untouched for the benefit of visitors, to whom he omitted leaving the key to unlock its coded mysteries.

Below
The mantelpiece in the small drawing room.

"Let the great myths of antiquity not be translated continually into the works of historiographers, but rather into those of the eternal poets, for we must escape at last from this puerile chronology that forces artists to depict finite time rather than eternal thought."
Gustave Moreau, quoted in *L'Assembleur de rêves, Ecrits complets,* **Gustave Moreau, preface by J. Palahide, collated and annotated by P.-L. Mathieu, Fata Morgana, Fontfroide, 1984.**

Books and mementoes in the small drawing room. Moreau was a passionate reader, his tastes including not only novels and poetry but also philosophy, and in particular the works of Schopenhauer. He maintained close relationships with numerous men and women of letters, including Jean Lorrain, Théodore de Banville, José-Maria de Heredia, Judith Gautier (daughter of Théophile), Jules Laforgue, Albert Samain, Robert de Montesquiou, Stéphane Mallarmé, and Joris-Karl Huysmans. All of these devoted either poems or prose writings to his works. And Moreau also wrote, leaving behind travel writings, memoirs, reflections on art, and, above all, a singular and impressive collection of dreams.

One of the second-floor galleries with, in the left foreground, the nine panels of *The Life of Humanity* (after 1879). The studios were laid out according to strict rules, in which Moreau set out to combine the spirit of a contemporary art gallery (with row upon row of closely hung paintings) with the apparent informality of a fictitious studio (with canvases displayed on easels, though always magnificently framed).

222

"My greatest effort, my sole concern, my
constant preoccupation is to steer as best
I can this yoke that is so difficult to drive
at a steady pace: my unbridled imagination
and my manically critical mind."

Gustave Moreau, quoted in *L'Assembleur de rêves,
Ecrits complets,* Gustave Moreau, preface by
J. Palahide, collated and annotated by
P.-L. Mathieu, Fata Morgana, Fontfroide, 1984.

the sixteenth and seventeenth centuries, dishes by Bernard de Palissy, and more faience from Moustier, China, and Japan.

The study or small drawing room was where Moreau painted, wrote, read, and received friends in his last years. Here he arranged belongings that had formerly been in his bedroom, and hung the walls with numerous watercolor landscapes that he had painted during his time in Italy in 1857–59. Alongside these hangs a selection of his best copies of old masters in the Louvre—works of the Italian school chiefly, but also some by Jan van Eyck and Velázquez. The bookcases are crowded with numerous treatises on architecture from the collection of his father, a prominent architect, with Flaxman rubbing shoulders with Piranesi and Philibert de l'Orme with Serlio and Percier. Plaster and bronze casts of treasures of classical sculpture mingle with Moreau's own contemporary works. He also managed to include his father's collection of ceramics in the Italian style and classical sculptures of great beauty, including a bust of Dionysus and a ceramic *krater,* or large dish, from the sepulcher of an Apulian princess. Finally he added a copy that he had made at the Accademia di San Lucca in Florence of a fragment of a Raphael fresco featuring a putto. The walls of the corridor leading to his private rooms are covered with Rembrandt engravings, drawings by Chassériau,

Berchère, and Fromentin, a fine Poussin, and reproductions of works by painters who had been important to him. Every detail of this remarkable space was designed to create an intensely evocative web of memories, with paintings and papers tracing obscure but parallel paths to the heart of a story told through a succession of subtle and esoteric associations.

In the spring of 1895, Moreau drew up his will, naming his friend Henri Rupp as his sole beneficiary. After Moreau's death in 1898, Rupp devoted himself to persuading the state to accept his bequest, committing large amounts of his own money to guaranteeing the upkeep of the future museum. Finally passing into state ownership in 1902, it opened to the public the following year under the directorship of Georges Rouault, one of Moreau's former students, who remained in the post until 1928. Other students from Moreau's studio at the Ecole des Beaux-Arts also made considerable contributions to the development of the museum, such as Emile Delobre, who took care of the framing. For many years the museum stood virtually unvisited, as Moreau's sumptuous work was overlooked in favor of another of his students, Henri Matisse. Only when his paintings gripped the imagination of the surrealists, as they had so many writers in his own time, would the legend and reputation of Gustave Moreau be sealed.

Opposite top (two pictures)
Two rooms on the second floor convey the impression
of visual saturation that Moreau sought. The
inventory drawn up between May 5 and November
28, 1898, listed some 20,000 items. The museum
opened to the public the following year, although the
state did not accept the bequest until two years later.
It remained financially independent until 1930, when
it was attached to the Réunion des musées
nationaux.

Opposite below
Detail of the staircase between the two studios.
When he embarked on his alterations of the house,
Moreau envisaged two studios one above the other,
planning already to turn them into picture galleries
for posterity.

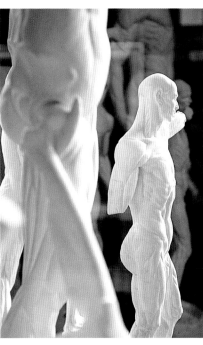

Left
Numerous plaster casts in the first-
floor studio. Although this studio by
this time bore no resemblance to the
one in which he actually worked,
Moreau wanted visitors to be able to
understand his artistic approach
through the objects and works that
inspired him.

Above
Detail of plaster casts.

WILLIAM MORRIS

Opposite and above (three pictures)
With Dante Gabriel Rossetti, Morris leased this lovely Cotswold stone manor house on the borders of Oxfordshire and Gloucestershire in June 1871. Called Kelmscott Manor, the house was the last residence of Morris. The state of his wife Jane's health had forced them to leave their marital home, Red House, which Morris had decorated. Soon after moving to Kelmscott, Morris set off on his first voyage to Iceland, a two-month journey in the company of his friend Charlie Faulkner, retired officer W.H. Evans, and his Icelandic tutor Erik Magnùsson.

Top right
William Morris.

Born in Walthamstow in East London, William Morris (1834–1896) went to Oxford University, where he developed his passion for the history and art of the Middle Ages. With his fellow student Edward Burne-Jones he founded a brotherhood opposed to the eclecticism of the Victorian age. Under the influence of Dante Gabriel Rossetti, Morris became part of the second generation of English Pre-Raphaelite artists. He very soon gave up painting, however, in order to devote his energies to two fields in which he displayed much more considerable talents: poetry and the applied arts. His marriage in 1859 to Jane Burden, whom he had met two years earlier, was to prove a turning point in his life. He decorated their home—the famous Red House in Bexley Heath—in the style that was later to become known as Arts and Crafts. Two years later, Morris founded the firm of Morris and Co. for the manufacture of furniture and fabrics reflecting the Pre-Raphaelite aesthetic. In 1871 he bought Kelmscott Manor in Oxfordshire. Here he continued his prolific work in the applied and decorative arts and founded one of the first private printing presses, the Kelmscott Press, while at the same time continuing to write poetry and romances, to make translations of old Icelandic sagas, and to campaign in support of socialism. So wide-ranging and far-reaching was his influence that he has an enduring reputation as one of the greatest pioneers ever to have worked in the field of the decorative arts.

"I have been looking about for a house for the wife and the kids, and whither do you guess my eye turns now? Kelmscott, a little village about two miles above Radcott Bridge—a heaven on earth; an old Elizabethan house like Water Eaton, and such a garden! Close down on the river, a boat house and all things handy, I am going there again on Saturday with Rossetti and my wife—Rossetti because he thinks of sharing it with us if the thing looks likely . . ."
William Morris, letter to Charles Faulkner, May 17, 1871.

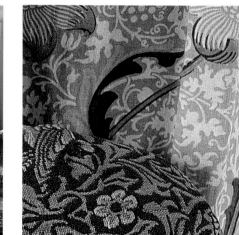

William Morris, manufacturer and poet, at Kelmscott Manor

William Morris's course in life was set very early on, when as a nineteen-year-old undergraduate student at Exeter College, Oxford, he displayed firmly held opinions and a passionate interest in medieval history, sparked by the overwhelming effect that the novels of Sir Walter Scott had on him as a child. At Oxford he met Edward Burne-Jones, and together they founded "The Brotherhood," with the aim of launching "a crusade and holy war" against the era in which they lived. He found echoes of these yearnings in John Ruskin's essays on art and in the poetry of Browning and Tennyson, and when he met the painter and poet Dante Gabriel Rossetti he was captivated. Joining Rossetti's Pre-Raphaelite Brotherhood forthwith, he resolved to become a painter. But after producing only a single canvas, *Queen Guenevere,* he changed his mind, deciding instead to choose the path of the applied arts and poetry. His work in both disciplines was to make him celebrated throughout the world.

Morris then fell hopelessly in love with Jane Burden, a young woman of unusual beauty whom Rossetti had spotted from a box at the theatre, and began to use as a model. In 1859, "Topsy" (Morris's nickname from his college days) married her. With married life begun, he engaged the architect Philip Webb to build him a large house surrounded by a garden containing a well with a gable-topped well-head, reflecting his own ideas, which ran counter to the eclecticism of

Victorian architecture. The result, though evidently inspired by late medieval Flemish architecture, was wholly original in style. Called simply the Red House, after the red of its bricks, the building formed a striking contrast with the lush green fields and hedgerows of the surrounding Kent countryside. While Morris made Webb responsible for the broad outlines of the internal decorations, he asked his friend Burne-Jones to help him in the making of the furniture, sparing no pains in his determination to create surroundings that were nothing short of idyllic. His designs encompassed everything from great press cupboards in the medieval style to stained-glass windows bearing his motto "If I can," and from tapestries to window hangings.

Forcibly struck by the irredeemable hideousness of the industrial products vaunted at the Great Exhibition of 1851, he had resolved then and there to bring about a revolution in the applied arts. This he did on a personal level in the form of the Red House, a tangible manifesto of his aesthetic ideals. But this achievement alone, symbolic though it was, did not support the declared principles of the Pre-Raphaelites to his satisfaction, and he was determined to find the means of doing so. Hardly had he finished work on the Red House than he founded, in 1861, the firm of Morris, Marshall, Faulkner & Co., Fine Arts Workmen in Painting, Carving, Furniture, and the Metals, known simply as "The Firm." Their aim was to produce furniture and decorative objects that

Right (two pictures)
Details of decorative pieces in the ground-floor
sitting rooms.

Below
In the small sitting room on the ground floor the
armchairs are covered with fabric designed by Morris,
again taking his inspiration from medieval designs.
In decorating Kelmscott he decided not to evoke the
Middle Ages as wholeheartedly as he had at the
Red House, but rather to adopt an approach of great
simplicity and relative stylistic purity. Furniture from
different periods rubbed shoulders with Morris's own
works designed for comparatively light and
uncluttered spaces.

"At this time the revival of Gothic architecture was making great progress in England and naturally touched
the Pre-Raphaelite movement also; I threw myself into these movements with all my heart, got a friend to
build me a house very medieval in spirit in which I lived for five years, and set myself to decorating it …"
**William Morris, letter to Andreas Scheu, September 5, 1883, published in Philip Henderson's *Letters of William Morris to
His Family and Friends*, London, 1950.**

Left
On the far wall of the small drawing room is a portrait of Jane Burden, Morris's wife. A wealth of paintings and drawings by fellow members of the Pre-Raphaelite Brotherhood, and especially, of course, Dante Gabriel Rossetti, covered the house walls, though Morris took noticeable care to avoid the claustrophobic clutter that was typical of the times.

Below
Motifs based on intertwined flowers and foliage were characteristic of Morris's style.

"Everywhere there was but little furniture, and that only the most necessary, and of the simplest forms. The extravagant love of ornament which I have noted in this people else-where seemed here to have given place to the feeling that the house itself and its associations were the ornament of the country life amidst which it had been left stranded from old times, and that to re-ornament it would take away from its use as a piece of natural beauty."
William Morris, *News from Nowhere*, 1890.

were inspired by medieval craftsmanship and flew in the face of neo-classicism, but at the same time avoided any hint of antiquarianism. Morris and his fellow workers were dedicated to the ideal of creating works of art that were also practical—of combining the requirements of beauty and utility in complete harmony. In its early days the company received a hostile response from potential commercial clients, and instead worked exclusively for churches. Gradually, however, it developed a broader clientele, and production expanded to include chairs, fabrics, and wallpapers as well as screens and stained-glass windows. Morris rapidly emerged as not only a tireless worker but also a courageous—though never reckless—company director. While there was room for the company to expand its activities he could not rest, and in addition to this managerial role he was also the principal designer responsible for the creative process behind their wares. But unfortunately—hampered possibly by his perfectionism and his outright rejection of modern technology—he was neither a shrewd businessman nor an efficient administrator. Despite the orders that flooded in, Morris, Marshall, Faulkner & Co. never managed to show a profit. Throughout all this intense activity, moreover, Morris managed to continue to find time for his poetic

In furnishing and decorating Kelmscott, Morris was at pains to preserve the original charm of the old manor house. In some places, as on the wooden staircase, he was content to arrange objects (here a tapestry, mirror, and clock) on whitewashed walls. It was an approach that demonstrated his awareness of the value of old buildings; as he wrote in his manifesto for the Society for the Protection of Ancient Buildings in 1877, "No doubt within the last fifty years a new interest, almost like another sense, has arisen in these ancient monuments of art; and they have become the subject of one of the most interesting of studies, and of an enthusiasm, religious, historical, artistic, which is one of the undoubted gains of our time; yet we think that if the present treatment of them be continued, our descendants will find them useless for study and chilling to enthusiasm. We think that those last fifty years of knowledge and attention have done more for their destruction than all the foregoing centuries of revolution, violence, and contempt." Morris was a pioneering voice in pointing out the dangers of the new enthusiasm for restoration.

Below
A van Eyck–inspired view of the staircase.

Far left
The first-floor passage.

Left
The garden viewed from the passage.

Below
Morris's desire to establish a close relationship between house and the surrounding garden is evident in this floral design by him in the first-floor bedroom. The patterns based on plants and flowers that were so dear to him formed part of his worldview based on a broad communion with nature.

"Everything made by man's hands has a form, which must be beautiful or ugly; beautiful if it is in accord with Nature, and helps her; ugly if it is discordant with Nature, and thwarts her."
William Morris, *The Lesser Arts*, 1878.

"…all the minor arts were in a state of complete degradation, especially in England, and accordingly in 1861, with the conceited courage of a young man, I set myself to reforming all that and started a sort of firm for producing decorative articles … and we made some progress before long, though we were naturally much ridiculed."
William Morris, letter to Andreas Scheu, September 5, 1883, published in Philip Henderson's *Letters of William Morris to His Family and Friends*, **London, 1950.**

Below left
The bedspread in Jane Burden's room, designed by Morris. Only in his own bedroom and his wife's did Morris give full expression to the strongly medieval-inspired decorative approach that he remodeled in a stylistic vocabulary not only of great richness, but also applied with virtuoso skill.

Opposite
On the canopy over Morris's bed is the following inscription, written by Morris and embroidered by his daughter May: *Rest then and rest/And think of the best/'Twixt summer and spring/When all birds sing/In the town of the tree/And ye lie in me/And scarce dare move/Lest earth and its love/Should fade away/Ere the full of day.*

"Simplicity of life, begetting simplicity of taste, that is, a love for sweet and lofty things, is of all matters most necessary for the birth of the new and better art we crave for; simplicity everywhere, in the palace as well as in the cottage."
William Morris, *The Lesser Arts*, **1878.**

work, publishing *The Earthly Paradise* to great popular acclaim. Indeed he was as prolific in this field as he was in his manufacturing firm, which had revolutionized the general perception of the "lesser" arts, and which was unmatched either within Britain or abroad.

In 1871 Morris made a far-reaching decision: while the mixed fortunes of his firm had not ruined him financially, he was obliged to reduce his expenses; and he wanted to find a house that he could share with his friend Rossetti. So it was that he left his tranquil haven in the Kent countryside for London, before moving to Kelmscott Manor in Oxfordshire, which had seduced him with its lovely old stone walls and mullions, its garden spilling over with roses and cottage-garden flowers alive with birdsong, and its setting among the woods and rolling hills of the Cotswolds.

His latest passion at this period was translating old Icelandic sagas, and for this he now planned a grand tour of northern Europe. But he was motivated by another reason, too—despite the birth of two daughters, his marriage was foundering. After the death of Rossetti's first wife, Jane had become increasingly close to him (some even maintained that Rossetti had convinced Morris to marry Jane in order to bind her to the Pre-Raphaelite brotherhood). Overwhelmed by despair, in 1872 Morris attempted suicide. What emerged from this unhappy situation was a fraught ménage à trois designed merely to save appearances in the prim and prudish atmosphere of Victorian England. There would be no happy ending to the complicated love story that was to unfold at Kelmscott Manor.

Deeply hurt, Morris increasingly withdrew into himself, throwing himself frenziedly into his work. He produced one translation after another, whether from old Icelandic or Latin (publishing a new translation of Virgil's *Aeneid* that caused a sensation), and penned long poems such as *Love is Enough*. Refusing all honors, including the chair of poetry at Oxford and the prestigious and coveted position of poet laureate, he instead turned his energies toward socialism, tempered by a somewhat utopian idealism as displayed in *A Dream of John Ball* and *News from Nowhere*, giving public lectures and participating in the First Socialist International. But his earlier projects still had a place close to his heart, and in 1888, with the support and collaboration of John Ruskin and Edward Burne-Jones, he founded the Arts and Crafts Society. Not content with writing, translating, designing chairs and tapestries, and overseeing the manufacturing

The walls of the main drawing room are papered with a Morris design based on grapevines and olive branches. Above the fireplace is a portrait of William Morris, and on the table lies a book printed and published by the Kelmscott Press. For Morris, the adventure of the Kelmscott Press was motivated by the desire to produce books with "a definite claim to beauty, while at the same time they should be easy to read and should not dazzle the eye, or trouble the intellect of the reader by the eccentricity of form in the letters."

and commercial activities of Morris & Co., which he had founded after buying out Morris, Marshall, Faulkner & Co., he now decided to turn his indefatigable energies to a new project: printing and book design.

In 1890, after making the acquaintance of the master printer Emery Walker, he founded the Kelmscott Press. As a collector of old books and manuscripts he already had a considerable knowledge and understanding of the printing process. He now bought a handsome printing press and installed it in his Hammersmith workshop. The lavish editions he produced there, large in format and printed on fine-quality paper, were inspired by the illuminated books of hours of the Middle Ages, and all carried illustration either by himself or by Burne-Jones. The most celebrated of them all remains the Press's edition of the works of Geoffrey Chaucer, with a specially designed Gothic typeface inspired by a fifteenth-century Italian model, decorative flourishes of intertwined foliage, and woodcuts by Burne Jones. The quality of all the materials used, including the sumptuous binding, was to assure the revival of a craft that had been in decline in industrial Britain. For subject matter Morris chose his beloved Icelandic sagas, the works of Rossetti, his own romances, and medieval authors including Chrétien de Troyes; altogether he was to publish sixty-four volumes in seven years.

William Morris died in 1896, worn out, according to his doctor, by the sheer exertion "of being William Morris, and doing more work than any ten men." None of his endeavors, either at Red House or at Kelmscott Manor, could be considered complete—but how could one man ever have brought such a quantity and variety of projects to fruition? Never a family home in the conventional sense of being devoted exclusively to private and family pursuits, Kelmscott was an enormous and inexhaustible laboratory of forms and styles. From it emerged a revolution in the whole of the decorative arts, which in turn gave rise to an infinite number of variations on art nouveau, from the American Liberty style to the Vienna Secession.

"We sat down at last in a room ... which was still hung with old tapestry, originally of no artistic value, but now faded into pleasant grey tones which harmonized thoroughly well with the quiet of the place, and which would have been ill supplanted by brighter and more striking decoration."
William Morris, *News from Nowhere*, 1890.

"We went in, and ... wandered from room to room ... to the strange and quaint garrets amongst the great timbers of the roof, where in old time the tillers and herdsmen of the manor slept, but which a-nights seemed now, by the small size of the beds, and the litter of useless and disregarded matters—bunches of dying flowers, feathers of birds, shells of starlings' eggs, caddis worms in the mugs, and the like seemed to be inhabited for the time by children."

William Morris, *News from Nowhere,* **1890.**

Above
Kelmscott Manor viewed from the garden. Although Morris occasionally expressed a desire to go back and live in a big city, he left Kelmscott only to attend to business matters and to go on his great voyages to the distant northern lands of Scandinavia (the last of these being to Norway).
He died at Kelmscott peacefully on October 3, 1896. His coffin was taken in a cart to the village church, which he had decorated for the parish harvest festival. Philip Webb, architect of the Red House—where Morris was happiest—designed his tomb in the little village graveyard.

Left
A Persian bird sculpture in the main drawing room.

Gabriele Münter
Selbstbildnis, 1935

GABRIELE MÜNTER

Opposite
The entrance passage.

Above
It was in June 1909 that Gabriele Münter and her lover Wassily Kandinsky decided to move to Murnau, "the home of Xavier Streidl, to the new house that Kandinsky fell in love with at first sight. He remained in love with it. He took time to consider it. He managed to convince me, and in late summer I bought the villa" (Gabriel Münter, *Journal*, 1911). In this house the broad outlines of the Blaue Reiter aesthetic were hammered out. Münter made a number of paintings of this house that was at once the symbol of a new artistic movement and the realization of her happiness. Like Kandinsky, she liked to paint the village of Murnau from the first-floor windows, with their views of the house rooftops, the church, and the castle.

Top right
Gabriele Münter in 1917.

After Wassily Kandinsky's departure for Russia and the outbreak of the First World War, Gabriele Münter (1877–1962) chose to stay on alone in her house in the small Bavarian market town of Murnau, which in the years leading up to the war had been one of the most lively and creative centers of avant-garde German art. For decades to come she continued to live and work in the house that she and Kandinsky chose together, and which little by little turned into a gallery devoted to the Blaue Reiter (Blue Rider) group of artists. All the women artists and virtually all the men who had helped to make Munich the unrivaled center of avant-garde art in the years after 1910 also came to Murnau, leaving behind works that gradually built up to form a gallery of the group's work. Even during the dark years of Nazism, Münter's work continued to develop in the solitude of this magical place, surrounded by the shades of artists whom the Third Reich had condemned as degenerate. She later donated the works she had managed to save—oil paintings, watercolors, and drawings by members of the group—to the city of Munich. By an ironic twist of fate, the municipality chose to house this unique collection in the house of another artist, the academic painter Franz von Lenbach (known principally for nearly 80 portraits of Bismarck), who had built a lavish Tuscan villa with a view to installing a gallery devoted to his own glory.

Right
The terrace.

Far right
In this substantial house, the artist busied herself with painting not only pieces of furniture but also wooden decorative features—as with the staircase—taking her inspiration from local folk art. By this period she had started collecting examples of Bavarian folk art, including the paintings on glass that heavily influenced her own work and Kandinsky's, and religious sculptures such as painted wooden statuettes of the Virgin. Some of these pieces appeared in one of her most striking paintings from this period, *Dark Still Life*, as well as in other compositions.

Gabriele Münter and the house of memories

On February 19, 1957, the day of her eightieth birthday, Gabriele Münter officially presented her collection to the city of Munich. It was an impressive collection, comprising twenty-five paintings and three hundred and thirty drawings by Kandinsky, together with works by other members of the Blaue Reiter group including August Macke, Franz Marc, Alexei von Jawlensky, and Marianne von Werefkin, as well as her own paintings. Münter obtained many of these works because she was the only artist from the group to return after the First World War to the little town of Murnau, not far from Munich, where she and her lover Kandinsky had lived together at the center of this revolutionary circle.

Kandinsky arrived in Munich from Russia in 1896 (the same year as Jawlensky and Werefkin), when the Bavarian capital and cradle of Jugendstil was one of the most exciting centers of artistic activity in Europe. There he rented rooms on Ainmillerstrasse, a mere stone's throw away from Paul Klee's lodgings, in the heart of the Schwabing district. Soon he started to make regular excursions into the surrounding countryside, taking with him students from the Phalanx School that he founded in 1901.

In 1904 he discovered Murnau, and immediately fell under the spell of its old church, its wooden houses painted in shimmering colors, and its seven idyllic little islands scattered across the Staffelsee lake. In 1908, just returned from a long period of traveling through Europe and North Africa, he spent six weeks at the Griesbräu boarding house, and the following year he decided to find a house there where he could spend the summer months, his choice eventually falling on the former Streidl villa at Dünaberg.

Born in Berlin in 1877, Gabriele Münter was twenty when she enrolled in the Damen Kunstschule (The Art School for Ladies) in Düsseldorf. Disappointed with the education she received there, she left for America the following year to visit relatives with her sister and stayed there until 1900. On her return to Germany, she studied with the Association of Women Artists and attended courses at the Phalanx School, where she met and fell in love with Wassily Kandinsky. Three years later—the fact that he was already married notwithstanding—they became engaged. Wherever he went she went with him, and she shared his love for Murnau.

The choice of this picturesque spot was not dictated solely by their shared delight in the Bavarian countryside, which the two of them frequently explored on long bicycle rides. At this time, Murnau was also one of the last remaining places where the practice of painting on glass was still carried out according to unique local traditions. Kandinsky, whose interest in all forms of folk art had been rekindled by his recent trip to Russia, was fascinated by this technique, which he not only learned but also applied with success to his own artistic vision.

Artistic life in Munich, meanwhile, was anything but dull, and Kandinsky took delight in causing scandal and outrage. When he put forward his *Composition V* for an exhibition staged by the New Association of Munich Artists in 1909, the jury rejected it, whereupon the artist stalked off in a rage and founded the rival Neue Künstlervereininung München (New Artists' Association of Munich), in which he was joined by Adolf Kanoldt, Jawlensky, Werefkin, Alfred Kubin and, of course, Münter. After two exhibitions at the Moderne Galerie Tannhauser, on December 20, 1911, Kandinsky resigned as president of the association after a quarrel with Jawlensky, who had formed a small breakaway group. This event was to prove the starting point for the remarkable Blaue Reiter group, founded by Kandinsky with Franz Marc and August Macke, and for a succession of intensely productive and happy summers spent at Murnau.

For several years Gabriele Münter had encouraged her fellow painters to make copies of and take their inspiration from the glass paintings of religious subjects, or *Hunterglasbilder*, for which the Staffelsee region was famous. It was this work on glass that led Kandinsky to question the necessity of representing objects in painting and then, by logical extension, to abstraction. At the same time, his growing interest in folk art encouraged him to experiment with increasingly bold color combinations. Murnau and the surrounding countryside offered Münter and Kandinsky the ideal

"We start from the idea that, in addition to the impressions that they receive from the outside world, artists also continually accumulate experiences in their inner world. They are engaged in a quest for artistic forms that should be free from all extraneous elements in order to express only the essential—in short, they aspire to an artistic synthesis that seems to be the watchword that presently appeals to more and more artists on the spiritual level."
Gabriele Münter.

Below
The traditional Bavarian wood stove on the first floor. It was at Münter's that the leading figures of the Blaue Reiter group would meet in 1911, on weekends and especially during the summer months. But Münter was difficult and unstable by nature, and soon fell out with Franz Marc and August Macke and their wives. Kandinsky was aware of this psychological frailty, which sometimes became evident in her work, and wrote to her several times exhorting her to show greater concentration, energy, and self-control. It was at this period, moreover, that their personal relationship began to suffer.

Following pages
Some works from Gabriele Münter's collection adorning the walls at Murnau. Outside the select confines of the Blaue Reiter circle, Münter and Kandinsky also welcomed young artists who would come to discuss their ideas about modern art. Münter took the opportunity to paint a portrait of one of these in *Man in an Armchair* (1913), later on describing the occasion in her *Journal,* "The first hot days of summer had arrived when one day in 1913 Paul Klee arrived wearing white trousers, which we greeted with joy as a sign of summer. Sitting in my big 'thinking' armchair, he was talking to Kandinsky when suddenly I saw the whole scene as a painting. I took my sketchbook, which I always have at hand, and discreetly made a rapid sketch. The white trousers were at the center of the composition, while the man, forming a right angle with the chair, merges with the paintings on the wall."

subject matter through which to express this new concept of space, and its depiction through the use of strong, clashing colors. Although not yet abstract, their paintings from this period display an exhilarating freedom in their use of figurative elements. At the same time, both artists began to feel increasingly distant from life in Munich, as Kandinsky later observed, "When I went back to Munich everything was in its place. It seemed to me that this was the true kingdom of *Beauty and the Beast*."

Münter's works from this period display a complete symbiosis with those of Kandinsky. Her *Dark Still Life* and *Kandinsky at a Table* (both 1911), and a number of self-portraits show a similar impulse to depict her surroundings through an emotionally charged use of contrasting colors, and to simplify her subjects to the extreme, even to the point of distortion. Their house became the focus for all those who explored these themes. The Blaue Reiter *Almanac*, to which Marc made such a large contribution, was drawn up here. It was here that the small group planned its exhibitions, notably at the Der Sturm gallery in Berlin in 1912 and at the Munich New Secession of 1914, where Jawlensky and Werefkin joined their number again. And it was here that Kandinsky, after writing his first manifesto, *Concerning the Spiritual in Art*, composed his first quasi-abstract compositions—his Improvisations— and wrote his first plays and his collection of poetry, *Klänge*.

With the outbreak of war in August 1914, the friends were forced to scatter; many fled to neutral Switzerland and Kandinsky returned to Moscow, while Münter went to Munich. Kandinsky never returned to Murnau, and eventually married the daughter of a Russian general. Münter, meanwhile, lived an unsettled life, working in various cities in Germany and Scandinivia until returning to Murnau where she lived with her partner, Dr. Johannes Eichner, from 1929 until his death in 1958. Münter continued to paint, while keeping in the basement of her house the shrine to the Blaue Reiter group, an impressive number of paintings, drawings, and engravings by these extraordinarily creative and original artists, some of whom, such as August Macke and Franz Marc, died at the Front. With painted staircases and furniture, and memories of Kandinsky and of her love affair with him, Gabriele Münter's house stands as a lasting reminder of a period of astonishing artistic innovation, by virtue of which Bavaria became one of the most vibrant and avant-garde centers of early twentieth-century culture.

Below
Self Portrait at the Easel, Gabriele Münter, c. 1911.

Below right
The Lyre, Wassily Kandinsky, 1907. Kandinsky remained profoundly influenced by Russian folk art, which provided an inexhaustible source of inspiration for him in his early Munich period. His later discovery of Bavarian folklore was to enlarge his artistic repertoire considerably and to enrich his style.

"A mass of hills in every color, which you want to depict and can depict. They are all different in size, but in form they are all the same; in other words there is only a single hill—broad at the base, swelling at the sides, and round and flat at the summit. Simple, ordinary hills, as we always imagine them but never see them."
Wassily Kandinsky, "Hills," *Klänge*, **1913.**

Opposite
A bookcase decorated by Münter. The artist cultivated the naiveté of Bavarian folk art not only in her decoration of furniture in the house but also in her paintings. It was a penchant that she zealously retained in her later work, even in her short-lived abstract period in the 1940s.

Blue, blue rises, rises and falls.
Something pointed, thin, whistled
And entered it but did not pierce it.
It rang in every corner.
Some thick brown remained, seemingly
Suspended for ever.
    Seemingly. Seemingly.
You must open them wider, your arms that you open.
    Wider. Wider.
Wassily Kandinsky, "Hills," *Klänge*, **1913.**

"Gabriele Münter is an exceptionally gifted artist. Her talent may be defined as purely feminine. There is no question here of fads or elegance on the cheap, nor of displays of masculine mannerisms (no vigorous brush strokes or pools of color splashed on the canvas). Her canvases are painted with the modesty of true artistic impulse. These still-lifes and landscapes have no other meaning and will always remain the expression of her spirit. Sincerity simultaneously attracts and reveals the sensitive soul of a woman."
Wassily Kandinsky, 1913.

JAMES ENSOR

The art of James Ensor (1860–1949) is deeply rooted in the life and atmosphere of the Belgian town of Ostend, where he was born. Its changing skies and beach frequented by wealthy sailors fired his imagination, as did its mesmerizing seas and its wild carnival, its narrow-minded bourgeoisie and its Flemish culture (which received scant attention at this period).

Ensor was also profoundly influenced by the family shop, still in existence today, where souvenirs, model boats, and exotic shells mingled with masks for the carnival—a delirious, iconoclastic time, at once joyous and tragic, when conventional values were abandoned for revelry. And there was also the influence of his family circle and the domestic setting, of a comfortable and conformist microcosm of oppressiveness and silences that were almost tangible. Eccentric in his spirit and paintings, Ensor tried his luck in both Brussels and Paris, but successive failures forced him to return to Ostend, where late in his career his talent was at last recognized and celebrated. While he depicted his own little world with savage humor and was happy to caricature himself, Ensor was also able to distill the microcosm of his domestic life and his studio into a vivid portrait in miniature of a whole society—with its traditions, legends, sensibility, vitality, and identity—in the form of his paintings, his drawings, and even his music.

Opposite
The harmonium in the drawing room, on which James Ensor composed and played his musical works, including *The Scales of Love*.

Above
The Ensor family shop, a mere stone's throw from the beach, now forms part of the museum devoted to the artist. In the late nineteenth and early twentieth centuries, when Ostend was a fashionable resort for European high society, the shop sold souvenirs to well-to-do tourists in the summer months.

Top right
Self-Portrait, James Ensor, 1884.

Right

A skull sporting a top hat on one of the shop shelves. Ensor's imaginative world was both bizarre and morbid, and he frequently evoked the medieval dance of death with his characteristically sardonic humor. As his work became ever more elaborate, the tension grew within him between the desire to sublimate the Flemish culture of which he was the deep-rooted product, and a solitary nature that indicated a profoundly melancholy disposition.

Below

The visitor to the James Ensor Museum today cannot help but be struck immediately by how the shop and its atmosphere appear to be frozen in time; most of the souvenirs and other items offered for sale to holiday makers of the belle epoque are still found here. Many of them served as models for the artist, whose fertile and inexhaustible imagination never tired of playing on objects from the familiar world of his childhood, when he was brought up by his mother, his grandmother, and his aunt, as they ran this shop.

"Ostend, paradise on earth and sea, Ostend, virgin of freshwater and saltwater, I carry you in the painted chapels of my dreams. Ostend, opal queen decked in mother-of-pearl, be ever pure and lovely in our eyes."

Speech by James Ensor on the occasion of his seventy-fifth birthday, 1935.

Opposite
Merchandise from the family shop, with items from Ensor's personal collection.

Left

Bizarre animals were an inspiration to the artist, who was strongly drawn to the fantastic and the macabre.

Below

The shop has been left as it was in Ensor's lifetime—a true cabinet of curiosities.

James Ensor, the recluse of Ostend

Although ignored for many years by his fellow citizens (if not dismissed as a madman), James Ensor expressed pride in his origins, though not without a hint of irony, "I was born on April 13, 1860, a Friday, the day of Venus. Well! . . . At dawn Venus came to me, smiling, and we looked long and deep into each other's eyes. Ah! Those lovely eyes, turquoise and green, that long hair the color of sand. Venus was blond and beautiful, and covered with foam. She gave off a strong scent of the salt sea." He was to spend nearly all of his very long life in Ostend, even when, late on in his career, fame, honors, and major European retrospectives brought him the recognition for which he no longer dared to hope.

He left the town of his birth only for a few years from the autumn of 1877 to 1880, in order to complete his studies at the Brussels Académie des Beaux-Arts. He did not much enjoy this period, however, dismissing the academy as a "school for myopics." But it was there that he met Fernand Khnopff and the critic, poet, and painter Théo Hannon, through whom he got to know the Reclus brothers; Camille Lemonnier, champion of naturalism; Félicien Rops; Ernest Rousseau; and the painter Willy Finch. Ensor's own work was in a realist vein, and had started to gain an appreciative response at modernist salons and exhibitions, though his one-man show in Paris in the winter of 1898–99 was a flop (one critic called his work "trash") and subsequently Ensor stayed close to Ostend.

Florent Fels, the art historian who visited the artist in his home shortly before his death, attempted to capture the atmosphere of the town, "A briny aroma everywhere told us that we were approaching his town and his sea. Women wearing dark veils like mantillas hurried along as though someone were chasing them down the streets of brick houses with crenellated roofs. In their clogs they scurried in the direction of the docks, oyster beds, salting sheds, markets, quays, and stalls on which the freshly caught plunder of the sea lay spread out . . . The sea spread its empire everywhere, lapping the docks marked out by rope-worn iron bollards, the light boats, the pilot boats, and the fishing boats bearing their nets stretched out at arm's length like lyres,

"I am very glad to have your opinion of my 'portrait with masks' and the compliments with which you are kind enough to flatter me. Who was the doctor who stood dumbfounded before the painting? Does he too have the viscous gaze of a slug swallowing its gall? In a mere twenty years the painting will be ready to be viewed by the always indisposed tribe of slugs and snails."

James Ensor, letter to Emma Lambotte, November 26, 1905.

Grotesque masks (such as these carnival masks from the belle epoque) and skeletons played a prominent part in Ensor's graphic imaginings. He was particularly fond of communal scenes featuring skeletons, as may be seen in drawings such as *Mirror with Skeletons* (1890), *Skeletons Warming Themselves* (1905), and *Skeletons Playing Billiards* (1903), and of course in paintings such as *Masks and Death* (1897). There was a close association in his work between the imagery of death and Flemish carnival masks.

Among the works hanging in the drawing room is a copy of *Skeletons Quarrelling over a Hanged Man* (1891), now in the Koninklijk Museum voor Schone Kunsten in Antwerp. Ensor painted his sister at the piano in a fine intimate composition entitled *Russian Music* (1881), and the same year used the drawing room as the setting for numerous paintings, including *Le Salon bourgeois*, *Portrait of the Artist's Father*, who is shown reading in an armchair by the fire, and *Portrait of the Artist's Mother*. Indeed there was hardly a room in the family home that he did not paint. Two of his intimate portraits depicting people in rooms of the house, *Lady in Distress* (1882) and *Dark Lady* (1881), prompted the novelist Eugène Demolder to eulogize, "The golden, powerful, sonorous song of the light captured in the great yellow lowered blind filtered through the curtains onto the velvets and covers! How keenly we feel the sky and the sun behind this serene closed window, and the lovely poem of warm light expressed in this simple act of waiting by an irresistibly pretty lady visitor!"

Following pages
Ensor often used puppets, such as these in the drawing room, as models.

Ensor painted portraits of members of his family, in particular his mother, Marie-Catherine, his aunt Marie-Louise, and his sister Mitcha in the drawing room. On the wall is a copy of *The Entry of Christ into Brussels* (1888), now in the Getty Museum, Los Angeles. Ensor's masterpiece was the culmination of a long and slow creative process, which he summed up in a speech he delivered on his seventy-fifth birthday in 1935, "In 1885, the series of the *Halos of Christ* or *The Sensitivities of Light*; in 1887, *Christ Rescuing St Anthony*; in 1888, *The Entry of Christ into Brussels* was the culmination of a very fine series around which ill-tempered claims swarmed in the mouths of anyone you care to name."

"The field of observation broadens to infinity, and a sense of vision, freed and sensitive to beauty, will constantly change and spy with the same sharpness those lines and effects in which shape and form are dominant. Yes, I have sacrificed wonders and dreams to the vermilion goddess."
James Ensor.

Far left
The large drawing room windows that feature in a number of Ensor's paintings.

Left
A characteristically macabre arrangement.

boats painted in bright colors so as to be visible in the northern fog. And as far as the eye could see, the infinite pink and gray horizon of the sea." These were the leaden skies and gray seas that inspired most of the works of Ensor's youth. As Fels observed, "Yet more skies, hard and devoid of all kindness or love; skies that were closed to you, poor, bare, and comfortless; unsmiling, official skies; all these skies, in short, only made your troubles worse." He also stressed the harshness and poverty of the coastline, "This was where our Nordic forefathers labored, crammed with vitamins, and their women, buxom or delicately Spanish. I think of the angry sea spitting its malevolence at them, of the relentless malice of men, of the treacherous buffetings of the harsh winds, tearing at our shelters built on courage and struggle."

The young Ensor's childhood was spent among women—his mother, his aunt, and his grandmother, who ran the family shop selling pets, lace, souvenirs, and books. As he later wrote in a letter, "I spent my childhood in my parents' shop, surrounded by strange creatures of the sea, by magnificent shells of pearly iridescence, and by the bizarre skeletons of sea monsters and marine plants." The austere women of his family inspired his first paintings of domestic subjects in 1881, such as *The Bourgeois Drawing Room* and *Afternoon in Ostend,* which showed his sisters sitting at the table, absorbed in their needlework. His younger sister, Mitcha, soon became his model, sitting for *The Dark Woman,* in which a woman all in black is shown seated on a chair in front of drawn curtains that hint at a hot sunny day outside, making a strange contrast with the chilly tones of the carpet and bed. Ensor's English father was a minor presence in this world of women, who soon after his marriage set off for America to make his fortune. Returning a ruined man, he sank into alcoholism and died in 1887. Ensor completed a deathbed portrait of his father, whom he admired despite everything and was always grateful to for having encouraged his art studies.

The souvenir shop, which Ensor kept just as it had always been long after his parents had died, like a shrine, would seem rather pathetic were it not for the significant part it played in the development of his art. Fels recalls the unimaginable riches of this Aladdin's cave with "porcelain figures of ladies bathing, ships in bottles, things made of mother-of-pearl, Chinese and Japanese china, grotesque statuettes . . . His major works were all set among this decor from his early childhood." Ensor's early still-lifes expressed his fascination for this magical place of baroque treasures and endless bizarre and wonderful objects. At a period when Whistler and Chardin both exerted an enduring influence on his work, he loved to evoke the pearly beauty of the shells on sale to tourists. In 1890 he painted *Studio Attributes,* in which he brought together a number of objects from the shop (particularly masks) and others from the family house (such as plates), combining them with an ancient sculpture and artist's tools. In his old age, Ensor recalled the shop as a place of enchantment: "In my parents' shop I saw the undulating lines and sinuous shapes of beautiful shells, the iridescent gleam of mother-of-pearl, and the rich tones of fine chinoiserie, and above all the sea, vast and constant, made a profound impression upon me."

The rooms of the family house, joyless and scrupulously tidy, presented him with the twin facets of the true nature of the Flemish people while also revealing to him the true nature of his art. An example of this expression is found in *My Favorite Room* (1892), in which a fireplace and a piano illustrate the methodical and predictable nature of Flemish society, while the paintings that cover the walls lend the room a jarring air of gaiety, as though the mission of these compositions was to transform the hard reality of life. For the small boy who found refuge in the attic (where he later installed his studio) the world of fantasy simply had to transcend this gray landscape, "Mysterious tales of fairies, ogres, and evil giants, dappled stories in shades of pepper and salt, gray and silver, also made a vivid impression upon me. Not to speak of that dark, scary attic, full of horrible spiders, curios, shells, plants and animals from faraway seas, fine porcelain, cast-off clothes the colors of rust and blood, red and

white coral, monkeys, tortoises, dried mermaids, and stuffed China-men." The masks on sale in the shop became an obsession and invaded his paintings, making familiar sights grotesque and terri-fying. He was completely infatuated with the Mardi Gras carnival, the scenes staged in this little theater of cruelty and fear, the practical jokes, and the merciless blows of fate that seemed to multiply almost to infinity.

It was the hilarious, uproarious excesses of the carnival, the frenzied cavalcade of grimacing, jeering masks, that inspired his masterpiece, *The Entry of Christ into Brussels* (1889), a huge canvas prepared with white lead and featuring doctrinaire flourishes, a large banner bearing the slogan *"Vive la sociale"* (Long live the collectivity) and a smaller one to the side reading *"Vive Jésus roi de Bruxelles"* (Long live Jesus, king of Brussels). Amid the confusion, the swirling movement, and the wild exultation, it is impossible to tell which of the pitiful, grimacing faces are masks and which are not. For many years the painting lay rolled up in Ensor's studio, until finally he decided to display it in the drawing room, so making a surprising addition to the otherwise impeccably conventional decorations. It was in this room that he also hung *Ensor at the Harmonium* (1933)—perhaps playing a tune from his *Scales of Love*, a ballet-pantomime in seven scenes, which had received its premiere in Ostend in 1913.

Ensor also painted a number of self-portraits. All of them, from *Self-Portrait of the Artist at his Easel* to *Ensor in a Flowered Hat*, show the same proud expression, but at the same time the portrait in the flowered hat recalls van Gogh's portrait of himself decked with lighted candles, which enabled him to paint at night. And each of these self-portraits reveals a change in his attitude as an artist. *Self-Portrait with a Big Head* shows an indecisive young man with a hint of arrogance that fails to conceal a streak of ambition; *Self-Portrait at the Easel* (1890) depicts a man of elegance and sophistication, turning to look at the viewer with neither haughtiness nor arrogance, but rather a comfort-able ease. The series of self-portraits in black, finally, reveals a man engulfed in shadows and mysteries. His studio was his realm of wonders, a world of pure imagination where he could toy at will with shadows and death.

"Ah! You should see the masks under our wide opal skies daubed with cruel colors, they wheel about wretchedly, their backs stooped, pitiful in the rain, terror stricken, simultaneously arrogant and timid, grunting and squealing, their voices shrill and falsetto or like wild bugle calls, heads of macabre creatures, inflamed joys, unexpected gestures, unruly as angry beasts. Humanity, repulsive, but so turbulent beneath its cast-off clothes, iridescent with sequins snatched from the mask of the moon."
James Ensor.

Opposite
Monet's kitchen. The artist chose the household's menus with meticulous care.

Right
Claude Monet in 1898, photographed by Nadar.

Below (two pictures)
The front door and a view of Claude Monet's house at Giverny. The aesthetic ideal pursued by Monet in his later life, as he transformed his house and garden into a natural paradigm of impressionism, transformed the little village of Giverny on the banks of the Seine into a place of pilgrimage—artists from throughout the world, and especially from America, were drawn to the wellspring of this new art, seeking inspiration in the model proposed by the grandfather of impressionism.

CLAUDE MONET

It was to his great longevity and his belated success as an artist that Claude Monet (1840–1926) owed the realization of his great dream, his house and garden at Giverny in France. No longer young and supple enough to dig trenches in the countryside in order to paint from a particular angle or in a specific light, he composed a garden of extraordinary luxuriance and beauty. Monet planned and planted it with skill and understanding, selecting plants and flowers, whether humble or exotic, to form color compositions according to the seasons and to suit his mood. By adding a large ornamental lake embellished with magnificent water plants and a bridge in Japanese style, he ensured the availability, literally on his doorstep, of many of the ideal subjects for his paintings—his great *Water Lilies* cycle being the most celebrated example. He also amassed a superb art collection at Giverny, including drawings, paintings, and sculptures by his friends, and also the finest collection of Japanese prints then in existence. Giverny thus became a sort of glossary of the impressionist aesthetic, created and constantly remodeled by the artist who was eventually recognized not so much as the leader of the impressionists, but as their most distinguished representative. Monet's fame transformed the small village of Giverny into a lively and picturesque colony of artists from all over the world, though chiefly from America, who made a considerable contribution to the quasi-mythical status now enjoyed by Monet and his work.

Painting and the gates of paradise: Claude Monet at Giverny

"In order to understand Claude Monet, his character, his way of life, his inner nature," observed art critic Gustave Geoffroy, "you have to have seen him at Giverny." No aspect of Monet's move to this house on the borders of the Île-de-France and Normandy was left to chance. "If only I had somewhere to settle," he would say, as he explored the Epte valley at length before embarking on the valley of the Seine. No, it was certainly not by chance that he fixed on this region of France. He had already discovered it in 1876, when he became a frequent visitor to the château of Rottembourg, the country house of Ernest Hoschédé, a wealthy and influential businessman who was also a great connoisseur of art, and who had bought several of Monet's paintings. Monet also paid several visits to his friend the painter Carolus-Duran, who lived near Hoschédé.

After Monet combed the area for weeks, he settled on Giverny. He was swayed in this momentous decision by a number of important considerations. Convenience was a major factor—from here Paris was within easy and rapid reach, as a little train ran on a branch line from Giverny to Vernon, where he could change for the capital. But most of all, he was seduced by the constantly changing skies, the captivating landscapes, and the proximity of the Seine, for he loved the water and was the proud owner of no fewer than four small boats. The two other rivers that meandered through the region also played their part in persuading him that this gentle green countryside was where he wanted to live. Marianne Alphant offers a perceptive analysis of the reasons behind his choice, "As at Argenteuil and Vétheuil, he was not mistaken, the instincts of the landscape painter obeyed the most ancient criteria for choosing a spot for a settlement—an intersection of valleys, a meandering river, and a geological fold to offer protection. Topographical perfection, biographical coincidence. Monet was precisely at the halfway point of his life. Stretching before him was not merely this great landscape punctuated with poplars, this orchard in blossom full of future promise, these blue hills on the horizon; the landscapes over which he gazed also contained the seed of an aesthetic adventure that was to last forty-three years."

The house that beguiled Monet had belonged to a merchant from Guadeloupe, who had lent it a vaguely colonial air that was all the more charming. It was of a good size, with four rooms on the ground floor, four bedrooms on the second floor, two attic spaces, a cellar, and a wing in which Monet could install his studio. He decided to rent it, moving in at the end of April 1883, just as news of the death of Edouard Manet

reached him. The year had already gotten off to a bad start, moreover, with the poor reception of his exhibition at the Durand-Ruel gallery; "A complete flop," he observed dryly. It was to be another seven years before he was in a financial position to buy the house. Times were very hard following the bankruptcy of his dealer, and matters were not helped by his own inability to make the slightest economy in his lifestyle (he still had two cooks at a time when his income was growing more and more sporadic and he had to provide for the education not only of his own children but also for those of Alice Hoschédé, whose husband had fled the family home after suffering a terrible reversal of fortune in 1877). But in 1889, at a joint exhibition with Auguste Rodin, he began to gain some recognition. This enabled him to carry out extensive works, building a second studio, enlarging the garden, and erecting a greenhouse for tropical plants. Subsequently he also enlarged the kitchen garden by buying the Maison Bleue on rue du Chêne.

He was painstaking in his attention to the garden, constantly sowing and planting new varieties of flowers, which—deliberately avoiding any architectural discipline—he arranged in the same way he would compose a painting. Geoffroy attempted to convey the sense of wonder that possessed him each time he visited Giverny, "As soon as you pushed open the little door, on Giverny's only main thoroughfare, you felt, at almost any season, that you had entered the gates of paradise. This was the realm of flowers, heady with color and fragrance. Each month was decked with flowers, from lilacs and irises to chrysanthemums and nasturtiums. Azaleas, hydrangeas, foxgloves, hollyhocks, forget-me-nots, violets, sumptuous blooms and modest flowers mingled and replaced each other in the soil, constantly and admirably tended by gardeners of the highest skill, under the infallible eye of the master." Among his friends, Monet reserved a special place for those who shared his passion for gardening. Among their number was Octave Mirbeau, journalist and art critic and tenant of the château de la Madeleine not far from Giverny, who wrote to Monet, "I am delighted that you have invited Caillebotte, we shall talk about gardens. Art and nature are mere nonsense. Earth is the only thing that counts. . . . I could spend hours looking at a clod of earth. . . . I love humus [decomposing plant matter] as though it were a woman."

As well as the garden, the lake was also enlarged and remodeled. Monet even obtained permission from the mayor to extend his garden to the other side of the railway line—prompting Georges Clemenceau to

The kitchen range at Giverny. It was the gourmet Monet who dressed the salad and served it at the table. He also had strong ideas as to how particular dishes should be prepared; asparagus should not be overcooked and porcini should be prepared with garlic and cooked in the oven with olive oil, and he always put the finishing touches to the wings of roast duck himself. He had his foie gras brought from Alsace and his truffles from Périgord, and deemed the wine of Chanturne indispensable for cooking haricot beans; his fund of recipes was inexhaustible.

Below

The *batterie de cuisine*. Monet had the greatest difficulty in finding a cook who was entirely to his satisfaction, and there was a high turnover of kitchen staff at Giverny. At last he found a true pearl among cooks in the person of Marguerite, who reigned unchallenged over the pots and pans, moulds, dishes, and ovens. Monet became so attached to her that when she married he engaged her husband as his sommelier in order not to lose her.

Right
The faience dresser in the dining room.

Below
A few Japanese prints from Monet's remarkable collection, the largest and finest in France at the time: Monet's knowledge of Japanese prints was that of a connoisseur, and his interest went beyond landscapes to embrace scenes from rural and urban life, scenes from the theater, and portraits of courtesans. In the late 1880s, he set aside landscape painting and concentrated on the female figure, and even found a model who suited him. But his wife, Alice, was furious, and threatened to leave the house if the model ever set foot in it. So Monet gave up his plans and returned to his customary subjects, never again attempting contemporary figure studies.

"In March sow grass seed, propagate the little nasturtiums, keep a close eye on the gloxinias, orchids, etc. in the greenhouse, as well as the plants in the frames. Put in place the borders as we agreed, and the metal wire for the clematises and the climbing roses . . . "
Claude Monet, letter to his gardener, 1900.

remark that he had his own private railway—and to divert the course of the River Epte in order to create a series of ponds. Willows fringed the lake, crossed by a Japanese bridge hung with wisteria, while the paths leading to it wound through a forest of bamboo, rhododendrons, and spruce. Another of the lake's decorative features, water lilies, were to become not only a source of boundless inspiration to Monet, but also one of his greatest and most audacious challenges, an achievement that was eventually crowned with the installation of the huge and highly decorative canvases in the Orangerie, a museum in Paris.

The countryside around Giverny provided Monet with two major themes in 1890, Poplars and Haystacks. The household of eight children, some belonging to Monet and some to Alice, who was to become his lawful wife only two years later, was already a subject of considerable interest to local people. Their surprise was even greater when they discovered Monet painting—with furious concentration—the trees that bordered their fields, and they promptly threatened to cut them down unless he paid them not to do so. When he turned his attention to their haystacks, the wily peasants again tried to blackmail him, threatening to dismantle the ricks if he did not give them money. Weary of all these hostilities, Monet spent more and more time in his garden, whose ever-changing beauty afforded him constant pleasure.

The household lived at a rhythm set by Monet, who every morning opened his shutters between four and five o'clock to scrutinize the sky. If the weather was inclement he might well return to bed, if only for the pleasure of getting up again. Breakfast at Giverny was in the English manner, adopted by Monet from his time in exile in London, and consisted of tea, milk, cheese, cold meats, eggs, grilled sausages, and bread and jam. Afterward he would work, either outside or in one of his two studios. At eleven o'clock he returned to the house, and lunch was at twelve. After a short break over coffee, he would return to work until dinner, served punctually at seven o'clock. No deviation from this timetable was allowed.

Apart from his painting and his increasingly rare journeys away from Giverny, his principal occupation and distraction was his unending string of visitors, as well as family visits, which on Sundays filled the garden with children and grandchildren. There were also his friends—Stéphane Mallarmé, Berthe Morisot, Paul Durand-Ruel, the Sisleys, Camille Pissarro (who for a while lived at Fragny-sur-Epte), Mary Cassatt (former pupil of Manet), Auguste Renoir, Caillebotte, and

Right
The kitchen from the blue drawing room. Monet received many visitors at Giverny, starting with the members of his family and his in-laws, whose numbers increased at an exponential rate. Art collectors and dealers such as Durand-Ruel and the Bernheim brothers were also frequent visitors. These visits invariably followed an unchanging ritual, starting with a visit to the studio, then a walk through the garden to return to the house.

Far right
The bookcase in the blue drawing room. Monet was a great reader who enjoyed the works of contemporary authors, some of whom were also his friends.

Below
The grandfather clock and Japanese prints in the blue drawing room.

Left
The simplicity of the decorations in Monet's house is remarkable in a period that favored showy and exuberant extravagance. Although the furniture he chose is of exceptional quality, it is distinguished nonetheless by its discretion and purity of form. Wicker chairs and chintz-covered couches created a comfortable, country-house atmosphere, seen here in the small drawing room viewed from the blue drawing room.

"In the winter, a greenhouse of medium size protects his precious chrysanthemums, single or double, and of all colors, golden and dark, above which there balances the fantastic, grimacing world of the orchids. In the heat, flowers bloom, mosses form carpets of green velvet, and water drips and babbles. It is an oasis in the midst of the sleeping countryside, silent in the snow."
Gustave Geoffroy, *Monet, sa vie, son oeuvre*, Grès, 1922.

Geoffroy, who introduced him to Clemenceau. Paul Cézanne came to stay at the Hôtel Baudy in Giverny in November 1894, only to leave without saying goodbye and without his paintings. And last there were the American artists who came on pilgrimage; the first was Theodore Robinson, who was kindly received. Then came Willard Metcalf, Frederick Carl Frieseke, John Leslie Breck, Richard Emil Miller, and Theodore Earl Butler, who married Alice's daughter Suzanne. The Hôtel Baudy underwent continual alterations in order to accommodate this rowdy colony of artists, gaining a tennis court and two studios, and even providing painting materials for its unorthodox guests. Soon there were no fewer than forty painters' studios in this formerly tranquil village, as artists from around the world came to Giverny to be part of the triumph of impressionism, including Radinsky from Czechoslovakia, Thornley from Norway, Watson from England, and Dice from Scotland. So great was Monet's reputation by now that one correspondent addressed a letter with the following ditty, "*Monsieur Monet que l'hiver ni/L'été sa vision ne leurre/Habite en peignant Giverny/Sis auprès de Vernon, dans l'Eure*" (Monsieur Monet, whose eye come wintry/Chill or summer heat ne'er errs/Lives and paints at Giverny/Near Vernon in the Eure).

Formidable in his energy for work, Monet was also a great reader, who loved to bury himself in the works of Balzac, Hugo, Tolstoy, Flaubert, Ibsen, Edmond de Goncourt, Zola (despite his disappointment with *L'Oeuvre*), Mirbeau, and Verhaeren. He also devoted a good deal of time and energy to his collections. His furniture—with the exception of

a few valuable pieces of Tuscan manufacture—might have been simple in the extreme, but his art collections were remarkable. Many of the works were gifts, such as a portrait of him by Carolus-Duran and some Rodin statuettes, and others were gained by exchanging his own paintings for works by friends and colleagues. Geoffroy took evident delight in describing Monet's bedroom, where he kept all his treasures, "This was not just a bedroom but also an art gallery, a museum of works by his fellow artists and those he admired. Around him he could gaze on an Italian landscape by Corot; four Jongkinds; . . . two watercolors and a thumbnail sketch by Delacroix; a sketch by Fantin-Latour; a set of drawings by Constantin Guys; two sketches by Boudin; four Manets; . . . a Degas, *The Bathtub*; two Caillebottes; . . . three landscapes by Pissarro; a landscape by Sisley . . ." The long list also included twelve Cézannes, nine Renoirs, five Morisots, a Vuillard, and a Marquet.

On top of all this, Monet had a passion for Japanese prints, putting together a collection that was beyond question the finest created by any artist at this period, outstripping the remarkable collection amassed in Antwerp by Vincent van Gogh. Monet claimed that his interest in woodcuts of the Edo period dated from his stay in 1871 in Zaandam in Holland, and Octave Mirbeau transposed this revelation to his novel *La 628-E8*, "During this trip I often thought of that magical journey on which Claude Monet arrived in Holland some fifty years ago to paint, opened a package to find the first Japanese print that he had ever seen. . . . Back at home and delirious with joy, Monet spread out 'his images.' Among the finest and rarest of them, though he did not yet

Sharaku portraits of actors in Monet's bedroom.

know it, were prints by Hokusai and Utamaro.... This was the beginning of a famous collection, but also—and above all—of a new development in French painting in the late nineteenth century." The story remains unconfirmed, but Monet used to enjoy telling it to friends and family. It is plausible, however, as one of the striking features of his painting entitled *Meditation: Madame Monet on the Sofa,* painted in the same year as Monet's trip, is its Japanese-style décor with fans and porcelain. Monet became a faithful client of Samuel Bing, who opened his gallery selling prints in 1879. Edmond de Goncourt remarked that the artist was "often at Bing's, in the little garret devoted to Japanese prints." Another visitor to Giverny was the scholar Tadamasa Hayashi, who advised de Goncourt on his monographs of Hokusai and Utamaro. Hayashi was also a dealer and a shrewd businessman who greatly admired impressionist painting, and Monet was able to exchange some of his works for wood engravings by Japanese masters both ancient and modern. Although his collection contained relatively few works by Harunobu, Monet managed to amass large numbers of prints by

Utamaro, Toyokuni, and Hokusai, as well as three splendid portraits of actors by Sharaku and a few late-nineteenth-century works in which foreigners begin to appear. Surprisingly, he took no interest whatever in the genre of prints known as *kosho-e,* or "birds and flowers."

Following the success of his *Rouen Cathedral* paintings in 1892 and his great voyage to Norway in the winter of 1895, Monet devoted himself exclusively to his garden and lake, the laboratory in which his art was created. As Marianne Alphant astutely noted, "For the 'studio visit'... Monet substituted a complex route, which in some mysterious way interwove his painting, his garden, and his house. There was no set itinerary, but a series of variations according to the season, the time of day, and the degree of intimacy." By the end of his long life, Monet no longer drew any distinction between his painting and his garden, the one reflecting the other in a play of mirrors that was as elating as it was frustrating for an artist such as Monet had always been, constantly dissatisfied with his work and striving for an ever higher degree of perfection.

Opposite and right

Water lilies and the Japanese bridge that Monet built crosses the lake fringed by lush vegetation. Octave Mirbeau, a close friend of Monet, wrote an ecstatic description of the gardens at Giverny, "It is spring. The wallflowers are giving up the last of their scent; the peonies, the divine peonies have faded; the hyacinths are dead. Already the nasturtiums and escholtzias are beginning to show, the former with the bronze-green of their young leaves, the latter with their strap-like leaves of a delicious acid green; and in the wide borders that they fringe against a background of orchards in blossom, irises display their strange curved petals tinged with white, mauve, lilac, yellow, and blue, evoking in their complex undersides veiled analogies, alluring, decadent reveries such as those that hover around the heady blooms of orchids . . ."

Below

Water Lilies, Claude Monet, 1904.

"Thus Monet's dream beside these deep waters will live on. It would be disastrous and unthinkable for this poem to be broken up, for these canvases forming a single composition, of which the viewer is the central point, to be dispatched around the globe in pieces, each of which could speak only as a fraction of a masterpiece. This will be a museum for the future, a museum without precedent or parallel, where future generations will come to muse on the poetry of the universe and ponder the immensity of the void."

Gustave Geoffroy, *Monet, sa vie, son oeuvre,* Grès, 1922.

ALFRED KUBIN

Alfred Kubin (1877–1959) suffered a wretched childhood and adolescence. Expelled from secondary school amid tragic family circumstances, he fared no better at the Salzburg School of Applied Art and was sent to work as an assistant to his uncle, a photographer in Klagenfurt, before attempting suicide on his mother's grave at nineteen. In 1898 he went to Munich to study art; there he saw Max Klinger's *Adventures of a Glove*, a revelation that led him to discover his own style. Following his first one-man show in Berlin in 1902, he exhibited with the Vienna secessionists. In 1904 he became friendly with Wassily Kandinsky, and two years later he met Odilon Redon during a stay in Paris. He then bought the house at Zwickledt in the region of Linz in upper Austria (present-day Czechoslovakia), where he lived with his wife, Hedwig, for the rest of his life. In 1911 he became a member of the Blaue Reiter group and began to gain a solid reputation. Virtually a recluse after the First World War, he did most of his work as a designer and illustrator at Zwickledt, in the process gradually transforming this quiet house into a library that is unique and an equally unusual museum.

"Frequently dreams are alarming omens, to which we all too easily remain deaf. Yet we should take such omens seriously, for in dreams we feel with more sensitivity and certainty than at other times. In dreams we whisper rather than talk, and the figures that loom up are to be guessed at and sensed rather than recognized and named. In the same way, it is only to be expected that such premonitions should come to artists, for the realm of dreams, of immersion in images from the subconscious, of enigmatic symbols engraved in objects and inviting deeper investigation—all this is familiar to them."
Ernst Jünger, *Rückblick*, 1949.

Opposite
The front door handle.

Below
Dried flowers hanging in the hall.

The haunted house of Alfred Kubin

Those who make the journey today to visit Alfred Kubin's handsome house at Zwickledt, hidden away in the lush green countryside outside Linz, have every reason to be surprised. Here everything radiates tranquility and harmony; neat, tidy, and bright, it could not be more at odds with Kubin's dark, tormented interior landscape. He wrote at length of his painful metaphysical quest, "Life is but a dream! Nothing seems more true to me than this celebrated phrase! The strange relationship that binds the diurnal and nocturnal spheres of our consciousness reveals itself, on sustained investigation, to be as surprising as it is familiar." Perhaps this opposition, between the darkness within and the placid countryside and picturesque building where he sought refuge from the wounds of history and the crushing demands of modern life, is merely superficial. And perhaps he also found need to seek solace in this typically Austrian house, a reflection of happier days under the reign of Franz Josef I, in order to withstand the savage assaults of his imagination. It seems likely that its reassuring quality was an indication of an imperative need within Kubin to find a safe haven and a protective cocoon.

The fates relentlessly pursued Kubin. Misfortunes seemed to rain down upon him during his childhood and adolescence. His mother died of tuberculosis in 1887, when he was just ten. Two years later, his father's second wife died while giving birth to his half-sister, Rosalie. His education was a disaster; after he was expelled from secondary school in Salzburg in 1890, he was then forced to leave his next attempt, the School of Applied Art in 1892 after a hopeless first year. His father, taken up with his own problems, sent the boy to learn photography; Kubin's uncle and teacher was the photographer Alois Beer. Kubin was extremely high-strung and subject to neurotic episodes that strained his relationships with both his colleagues and his superiors; in 1896 he ran away and found his way to his mother's grave at Zell am See, where he unsuccessfully attempted suicide by shooting himself with a revolver. After this unhappy episode he managed to enlist in the army, but after only three weeks of garrison life he finished up in the military hospital at Graz, suffering from a nervous breakdown. In 1903, on a visit to his father at Schärding, he met and fell in love with Emmy Bayer, and fortune at last seemed to

Right
View of the hall from
the dining room.

Below
View of the dining room
from the passage.

smile upon him; within a few months, however, she lay dead of typhus fever.

A year later he married Hedwig Gründler, sister of the writer Oscar A.H. Schmitz, but she too fell gravely ill in December of that year, and suffered from numerous relapses in the years to come. After all this, the death of his father in 1907 came as a crushing blow. In the first of a series of autobiographical essays, completed in 1911, Kubin described his despair, "I have still not managed to overcome the shattering pain of this loss, and I have to make a great effort to suppress all the emotions associated with it. The feeling of truly touching the void that I experienced at the time of this calamity has marked me so profoundly that neither changes in my fortunes nor conscious reflection will ever be able to change it." To add to his woes, his wife was taken ill again and had to go away for a course of treatment. In 1914, after a trip to Paris that proved on the whole both pleasurable and instructive, he was prostrated by the outbreak of war, which cast an implacable shadow over his view of the world. News of the death at the front of his friend Franz Marc, whom he had known in Munich, and of a female friend in France, undermined his already fragile mental state still further.

Worse was to come. In 1916 he was struck with full force by what he described as a "breakdown of morale" in one of the worst episodes he had yet endured. "I shut myself away from my friends and family, even from my wife, and broke off all correspondence with them, and I made arrangements of an extreme nature regarding my property, which like my art had become quite foreign to me, a matter of complete indifference. My wife asked me at least to sleep in the house, and so I turned a small corner into a 'cell' containing only a straw mattress and a washstand." For ten long days he lived in total isolation and suffered hallucinations. "In this state of permanent ecstasy I saw extraordinary things, similar to those I had often before imagined for my drawings and which are more or less attributed by legend to the vision of St. Anthony."

A reading diet of the tales of the Brothers Grimm and Buddhist sacred texts, combined with breathing exercises, afforded him some respite at times, and at others only sharpened his anguish. "Often there resonated within me the continuous sound of footsteps of every sort, drawing closer and then receding, or else it was a humming noise, or the cries and moans of a great crowd of people. When I talked

"The world is like a maze to me. I would like to find my way through it, and as a draftsman I should do so. Since I was a child, visions and evocative images have played an essential part in my life; they used to enchant me, and sometimes they made me tremble. I would like to keep a hold on these insubstantial, incomprehensible creatures. But the source of this phenomenon is of little concern to me. An irresistible impulse compels me to draw figures that spring from the shadows of my soul. How to pin down a constantly moving image in a drawing? By practice! Lost in contemplation but active as an artist, I analyze the vision, reconstruct it, and attempt to create a clarified image of my dream."

Alfred Kubin, *Construction and Rhythm*, 1924.

Left
The upright piano against the plain wood paneling of the dining room.

"Life is but a dream! Nothing seems to me more true than this celebrated phrase!
The strange relationship that binds the diurnal and nocturnal spheres of our
consciousness reveals itself, on sustained investigation, to be as surprising as it is
familiar. Each of these spheres is the touchstone for the other! The close relationship between the identities of the 'creator' of the dream and of his 'creature,' the
dream image, emerges with particular clarity in the field of dreams."
Alfred Kubin, *My experience of dreams,* **1922.**

to people, everything took on a double meaning, and the most
ordinary, mundane things became extraordinary; stones, mounds of
earth, tree trunks, and other similar objects seemed to me to display
such prodigious artistic qualities that, although in my heart I felt
something gentle and joyful, I hardly dared to look at them; all these
objects appeared to me like ghosts and masks jeering at me." The
deeper he plunged into meditation and mysticism, the more he fell
victim to attacks of acute paranoia and incurable insomnia. Then at
last he received a revelation; abruptly rejecting Buddhism and halting
his exhausting exercises, he simply returned to his normal way of life
as if absolutely nothing had happened. Now he experienced a feeling
of completeness and even a sort of happiness. "Since that time," he
confessed, "I have experienced not only the most serene, but also the
happiest and fullest moments of celestial joy."

After the Armistice and the dismemberment of the Emperor Franz
Josef's empire in 1918, Kubin, although deeply affected personally by
these momentous events (as he had been born to a German-speaking
family in northern Bohemia who had moved to Salzburg in 1879,
Austria was virtually his homeland), Kubin rejoiced that the universal
dance of death was at last over. And with the declaration of peace
came developments that brought considerable satisfaction in his

professional life: his first retrospective in Munich, the first indications
of official recognition, and the dominant position now enjoyed by
Germanic art, which was to continue unabated until the Anschluss
and the next war.

Kubin's acquisition of his fine house in Zwickledt thus corres-
ponded to a time in his life when a number of different factors
representing the fundamental poles of his existence came together.
In the wake of a period of intense and productive activity, he had
experienced great difficulty in developing his art further, as he
recalled in his autobiography, "I found myself in a state of deep
depression, and when my father drew my attention to an opportunity
that had arisen to buy a small house close to the River Inn in Upper
Austria, I was won over by the idea. The fact that my artistic dilemmas
had made the atmosphere of Munich unbearable to me made it all the
more appealing. That was when we moved to Zwickledt, where we
have lived ever since." The many problems that he had endured in
Munich had made life there virtually intolerable for him. Yet Munich
had also had a great deal to offer, as it was there that he met Max
Dauthendey, who gave him an introduction into intellectual circles;
Hans van Weber, later his first publisher; members of the Secession
who invited him to exhibit with them in 1904; and Wassily Kandinsky,

Far left
View of the small drawing room from the landing.

Left
View of the landing from the small drawing room.

Below
The small drawing room with the studio beyond: in marked difference to painters' studios, Kubin's studio featured a large table and shelves for storing drawings, engravings, and different types of paper.

Kubin's work table
in the studio.

Below
The studio: the tranquil
world of a tormented soul.

"What I like about your drawings it is not just their poetic spirit and their lively
and masterly technique, which never becomes a bravura exercise. I also feel a
great closeness to them. I imagine their birth to be like that of my poems:
generally during the course of a sleepless night, with hands scribbling and
doodling on sheets of paper balanced on your knees.... Even if it is neither at night
nor in bed, this is how I imagine many of your drawings coming into the world.
From the obsession or enchantment with a subject or image and the exhilaration
of the lines or strokes there emerges something completely spontaneous and
unplanned. It is a very serious game, as only true games can be; a seriousness that
is so light that it appears weightless, and hangs in the air like a soap bubble."
Hermann Hesse, letter to Alfred Kubin, April 1942.

"At the moment of original conception I am driven by an
obscure impulse, but for the completion of the work both
hand and eye must work with much greater precision and
subtlety; in this work I submit myself completely and
unreservedly to the workings of my conscious mind."
Alfred Kubin, *Creating from the Unconscious*, 1933.

Right
Right
Kubin's lead pencils: he
used color only as
accents on his drawings.

Below right
A corner of the studio.

"Deep down all is fantasy. The artist is only one of the countless reflections of the power of the divine imagination; the more a work overflows with imagination, the greater will be its importance on earth. This degree of significance is not immediately evident, of course. To gain a greater understanding of it, we must surrender to the surging power of the soul, not merely in an active manner but also by submitting to and being possessed by the very essence of the power of the divine imagination born of the individual. All the mystery of creation and the magic of the moment are then revealed."
Alfred Kubin, *Confession*, 1924.

who invited him to take part in the Phalanx School exhibition. He maintained his ties with this city, which was now a mecca for avant-garde artists, enrolling in the Neue Künstlervereinigung München in 1908, and taking part in the exciting Blaue Reiter venture alongside Kandinsky, Gabriele Münter, Jawlensky, Marianne von Werefkin, and Franz Marc. It was in Munich, finally, that he had his first one-man show, at the Galerie Tannhauser in 1913.

Whatever the case, Kubin observed that from the moment he shut himself away at Zwickledt his work took off in unprecedented fashion. The decision to buy this house beyond the Werstein had of course been made with his wife, Hedwig, on whose presence he relied for his mental stability and also for his ability to work, constantly threatened as this was by his tempestuous inner life. And it was here, despite bouts of depression, that he managed to rekindle an interest in the world outside, as for example after the death of his father. "I abandoned myself to observing my pets and other animals: an extremely lively monkey, a tame roe deer, cats, aquarium fish, and a collection of beetles. I spent hours wandering in the forest and through the fields, and gradually I took up my pencils again and filled a dozen notebooks with my whims . . . I spent the spring and summer engaged in such occupations." But after a journey to northern Italy with his friend Fritz von Herzmanovsky, he found drawing was no longer sufficient to express his emotions.

It was in 1908, in the house haunted by his dreams, that he started work on his first and only novel, *Die Andere Seite (On the Other Side)*, completing it in eight weeks. He took another month to do the illustrations, reusing in part the drawings he had done the year before for Gustave Meyrink's *The Golem*, which the latter had been unable to finish. Even before his arrival in Munich, Kubin had taken a great delight in literature and philosophy. It seemed quite logical that he should want to illustrate his favorite authors, both classic and contemporary. The first opportunity to be offered to him in this field was the design of the frontispiece for Thomas Mann's *Tristan* in 1903. From this point on he earned a considerable reputation as an illustrator, working constantly on one great literary text after another, in all genres and from every historical period. Notable examples

included *Aurélia* by Gérard de Nerval, *Tales of the Night* by Edgar Hoffmann, *Lesabèndio* by Paul Scheerbart, *On the Marble Cliffs* by Ernst Jünger, *The Thousand-and-One Nights,* the poems of Georg Trakl, *The Adventures of Baron Münchhausen* by Rudolph Erich Raspe, *The Double* by Fyodor Dostoyevsky, *Les Diaboliques* by Jules Barbey d'Aurevilly, *Death of a Petit-Bourgeois* by Franz Werfel, the works of Hermann Hesse (who became a friend in 1928), books by Edgar Allen Poe, and the works of Jean-Paul Richter. He also worked on projects based on the Bible with other members of the Blaue Reiter group; his twenty illustrations for the Book of Daniel were not published until 1924.

At the same time Kubin continued to write his tales of fantasy and essays on art, and he was a prolific letter writer. He owned a remarkable library, which was preserved with his archives with the utmost care during, and especially after, the Second World War. Kubin was delighted at the overthrow of the Third Reich, but the last days of the war did not spare peaceful little Zwickledt, as he recalled in his autobiography, "The bombing of the night of May 1 to 2, 1945 claimed the sacrifice of three lives. . . . I had put only my original drawings in a safe place, but we were lucky, because the old house was badly damaged all the same by a hail of grenades . . . " At the time, his precious archives were in Hamburg, which suffered devastating bomb damage. Fortunately their custodian, Kurt Otte, had the foresight to store the thirteen boxes in the basement of the city's public library, and the fire that raged through the building caused them only minor damage.

In 1955, Kubin, friend and contemporary of Kafka, made a gift to the state of Austria of his own works, his library, and his house, which over a period of fifty years had witnessed the creation of thousands upon thousands of drawings, each more disconcerting and unexpected than the last. Three years after his death in August 1959, with every precaution being taken to preserve its distinctive atmosphere as far as possible, the museum that we see today was set up within its walls.

Above
The Night Walker, Alfred Kubin, 1904. Kubin's graphic world was peopled by monsters and phantoms, fantastical creatures and frenzied scenes, generally depicted in monochrome, with very little use of color. Although his work may be likened to that of Odilon Redon and Félicien Rops, it is less precious than the former and more restrained than the latter. Kubin also displays a greater intimacy with death than either of his great predecessors.

Opposite
Working materials on shelves in the studio.

Following pages
The bedroom where Kubin died in 1959.

Below

The library, with the small drawing room and the studio beyond. Literature played an important part in Kubin's life. Not only did he illustrate numerous works, both ancient and modern, but he also wrote a novel, *Die Andere Seite* (The Other Side), which enjoyed considerable success within the German-speaking world and beyond, and a large number of novellas, which were published at irregular intervals until his death. These writings form an extension of and indispensable companion to his graphic works, and he frequently expressed his desire to illustrate them.

"During this time before us today, as before the old masters, there stretches the ocean of the world—a vision charged with enigmas of all kinds, its infinite surface glittering with thousands of reflections inviting the artist and designer to continue their liberating action."
Alfred Kubin, *Bilan*, 1949.

Bottom right
A pair of armchairs in the library.

Bottom left
A part of the bell pull in the library.

Right
The small drawing room, with the library beyond.

GIORGIO DE CHIRICO

Opposite
The whole of the first floor in the Rome apartment, arranged as one large reception space, is decorated with limited edition late bronze statues by de Chirico, such as this one in the drawing room.

Above
The apartments enjoy an enviable position, looking out on one side over the Piazza di Spagna and on the other up to the two cupolas of the church of the Trinità dei Monti and the French Academy in the Villa Medici. Only after long and laborious searching did the artist and his wife manage to find this exceptional place to live.

Top right
Giorgio de Chirico.

In 1909 Giorgio de Chirico (1888–1978), standing before the statue of Dante in Florence, experienced the vision that changed the course of his artistic career. Forsaking the mythological subjects inspired by the work of Arnold Böcklin on which he had concentrated previously, he turned to painting metaphysical squares charged with an uneasy atmosphere of mystery and strangeness. During his time in Paris, his paintings attracted the admiring attention of Guillaume Apollinaire and gained a reputation as works of startling originality. After the First World War, with Alberto Savinio (his brother), Carlo Carrà, Filippo de Pisis, and Giorgio Morandi, he invented the movement known as the Metaphysical School, and established strong links with the journal *Valori Plastici*. Returning to Paris in the 1920s, he was at first adulated by the surrealists before being denounced by André Breton over an obscure matter involving a sale to the collector Jacques Doucet. The rift was definitive, and de Chirico returned to Italy. But already he was planning to explore another genre, a highly ambiguous "return to his craft." The late works that remain in the vast rooms of his Rome apartment reflect the dominant spirit of his work from the 1930s onward—pastiches of old masters alternating with ironic self-parodies of his own metaphysical world, as though he had set out to reconcile the old with the new—and are all set against a slightly unreal decor reminiscent of a 1950s film.

Below

The first floor drawing room and antechamber with de Chirico's eclectic mix of furniture: this antechamber still contains two of the artist's self-portraits, one in seventeenth-century costume and the other completely naked. In his work, the highest forms of painting were inseparable from a spirit of irony. The writings of his wife, Isabella Far, give credence to the idea of de Chirico waging a crusade against modern art in all its manifestations. As she wrote in *Portraits and Still Lifes*, "Today painting is no longer a great art. Painting today is all decoration and prints . . . "

Opposite

The rooms adjacent to the drawing room form the reception area where he installed a large collection of post-war paintings that reveal his unusual approach to art, expressed in his references to the metaphysical themes of the years after 1910 and the return to workmanship of the 1920s and 30s. During his lifetime he attempted to donate this exceptional collection to the Galleria Nazionale d'Arte Moderna in Rome, which turned it down.

Giorgio de Chirico's studio touching the Roman sky

"The place in the Piazza di Spagna was worth renting in every way, especially because of its central position. We are close to all those places and shops that we more or less need to frequent. In the Piazza di Spagna there are first-class chemists, banks, international bookshops, travel agencies, dispatch companies, high quality hairdressers, art galleries, shops selling things for men and women, etc."

Giorgio de Chirico, *The Memoirs of Giorgio De Chirico*, 1962.

Giorgio de Chirico returned to Rome in 1945, after living in Florence during the Second World War. He found a small furnished apartment right in the heart of the Eternal City, on Via Mario de' Fiori. What he really liked about these lodgings, which he described as "dark and dismal," was the reputation of the street they stood on, a favorite place for prostitutes to ply their trade before the new laws shut down the city's brothels. When he heard of an apartment to let in nearby Piazza di Spagna a couple of years later, he rushed around to see it and moved in immediately with his wife, Isabella Far, and a few essential items of furniture. After carrying out major works and, as he wrote in his *Memoirs*, "disinfecting it throughout, as it was crawling with cockroaches of all sizes and colors," he could appreciate at leisure the apartment's exceptional position, commanding magnificent views of the back of the church of Trinità dei Monti, and of the front of the famous piazza with its fountain by Bernini. Down at street level, meanwhile, he could relish the cosmopolitan bustle of the Trident, the three roads leading to the Piazza del Popolo, thronged with artists and art dealers as well as travelers. At the top of Via Condotti lay the venerable and celebrated Caffè Greco, where he could regularly be found grooming his notoriety and basking in the glory of a life's work now behind him. In *Nostalgia for an Autumn Afternoon*, de Chirico described his weakness for city centers, "I have always tried to live more or less in the center of cities, and I have always had an absolute horror of the suburbs. So in Paris I lived for a while on rue Meissonier; in Milan on Via Gesú, virtually on the corner of Via Montenapoleone; in Florence for a time on the Piazza della Repubblica, formerly Piazza Vittore-Emmanuele II, and so on elsewhere."

The couple's designs for their new home were unusual, to say the least. The first floor consisted of an outsize salon, furnished in Louis XVI style and divided into a drawing room and a dining room. The drawing room was itself subdivided, as though intended for lavish

"It does not even occur to the modern connoisseur that a painter should above all else be a work of art. He believes that the painting is an image, and that its value depends solely on the subject it depicts. Thus today's connoisseur obediently accepts melancholy, muddy landscapes, nonexistent still lifes, and empty, shapeless figures."
Giorgio de Chirico, *Monsieur Dudron*, c. 1945.

Below
One of the first-floor rooms hung with paintings from the artist's collection. The choice of paintings was dictated by de Chirico's desire to provide a résumé of virtually every phase of his long artistic career. From metaphysical squares to enigmatic dummies, and from still lifes to mythological scenes in which he amused himself by returning to the old masters, the visitor to these grandiose rooms is offered a panorama of de Chirico's development in just a few minutes.

receptions or large and fashionable parties. Scattered with sofas and armchairs upholstered in pearl-grey (a striking contrast with the vivid red of the curtains), oriental carpets, eighteenth-century furniture, baroque sculptures, and modern coffee tables, this procession of rooms was more like a select gentlemen's club than the home of an artist who, though now established, remained nonetheless fairly wild and outspoken. While it was reserved for de Chirico's social life, this floor was also his picture gallery. Here he hung some fifty of his paintings from the 1950s, harking back to his work in Paris in the years after 1910, the metaphysical paintings of his Ferrara period during the First World War, and portraits of himself either in costume or completely naked. Other works were unabashed plagiarisms of works by Rubens, Delacroix, Courbet, and many other old masters, just as he plagiarized himself—probably in a spirit of irony and willful mystification, and doubtless in the full conviction that he was already (and had been for many years) a member of this illustrious pantheon.

Small bronze sculptures depicting recurrent themes were scattered here and there, on tables, consoles, and chests of drawers. But nowhere in the apartment was there a single painting by any of the masters whom he admired and studied, and about whom he had written so much and so well, let alone by any of his contemporaries. It has to be said that once the war was over, de Chirico only stepped up his own personal war against art dealers and forgers, denouncing some and being taken to court by others. He also launched attacks on critics,

Opposite
The last room on the first floor contains works from de Chirico's personal collection. The sculptures and paintings are from his last period. Modern-art specialists have severely criticized de Chirico for his repetitions of the Piazza d'Italia and the metaphysical paintings. This was, in fact, a highly iconoclastic strategy on his part that was also intended to frustrate the schemes of speculators who valued only his paintings of the period from 1910, to the exclusion of all others.

Opposite

The grand enfilade of rooms creates a highly formal
impression. While de Chirico's metaphysical compositions are one of the cornerstones of twentieth-
century art, they are nevertheless marked (like his
brother Alberto Savinio's plays) by a deep-seated
nostalgia for classical antiquity and the Renaissance.
This past is revisited constantly in his work, through a
variety of forms of expression. The choice of furniture
in these rooms reflects this constant desire not only
to bring together different periods, but also to cast
the rich shadow of the past over the present.

journalists, and any artist who felt justified in producing modern "daubs." In his eyes this space, designed (one might imagine) for the decorous exchange of ideas, was in fact a gladiatorial arena, a battleground on which he was determined to outflank his enemies.

The floor above, which was the top floor of the building, housed the bedrooms of de Chirico and his wife as well as his studio. His bedroom was like Napoleon's, cramped and Spartan, with only a narrow bed and the bare minimum of furniture. His wife, by contrast, found herself in a considerably larger and more comfortable room furnished with considerable style. For de Chirico, the place in which he slept was of little importance (even if dreams played a role of crucial importance in both his art and his writing, as is clear in his two works of fiction, *Hebdomeros* and *Il Signor Dudron).* In his *Memorie della mia vita* he drew a discreet veil over anything that touched upon his private life, and vouchsafed not a word about the decor of his last home. But when it came to describing his studio, with its bookcases and its glorious views, he was unstoppable. "My studio, on the fifth floor, is magnificent. From the terrace I can often see superb effects in the sky, clear skies and misty skies, glowing sunsets, moonlit skies, night skies with clouds outlined in pale yellow, as in certain seascapes of the Dutch and Flemish schools. My pencil and paints are always at hand so that I can quickly record

these natural spectacles, and these sketches are useful to me later when I work on my paintings." Essentially a painter of landscapes of the mind, of metaphysical scenes in which elements borrowed from the world of reality invariably assumed another dimension and a different meaning, de Chirico never worked from life, unlike Corot whose work he greatly admired.

If a home can be assumed to reveal a great deal about its owner, it seems abundantly clear that the apartment on Piazza di Spagna was a world apart from the skillful construction of Mario Praz's *House of Life*, which wove secret connections between the works of art and the objects in his collection. De Chirico allowed nothing personal to show through, except perhaps for lavish tastes and an attachment to a sublimated past hedged by myths, almost certainly because he had hoped for so long for an official recognition that never came. The paintings that visitors see today, in what is now the Isabella and Giorgio de Chirico Foundation, are the gift that the artist wanted to make to the National Gallery of Modern Art in Rome; but a last bitter humiliation awaited him, as his gift was turned down by the minister of culture and the museum's board of directors. This is the melancholy reason why the paintings still hang here in these grandiose rooms, where de Chirico's metaphysical mysteries do not seem entirely out of place.

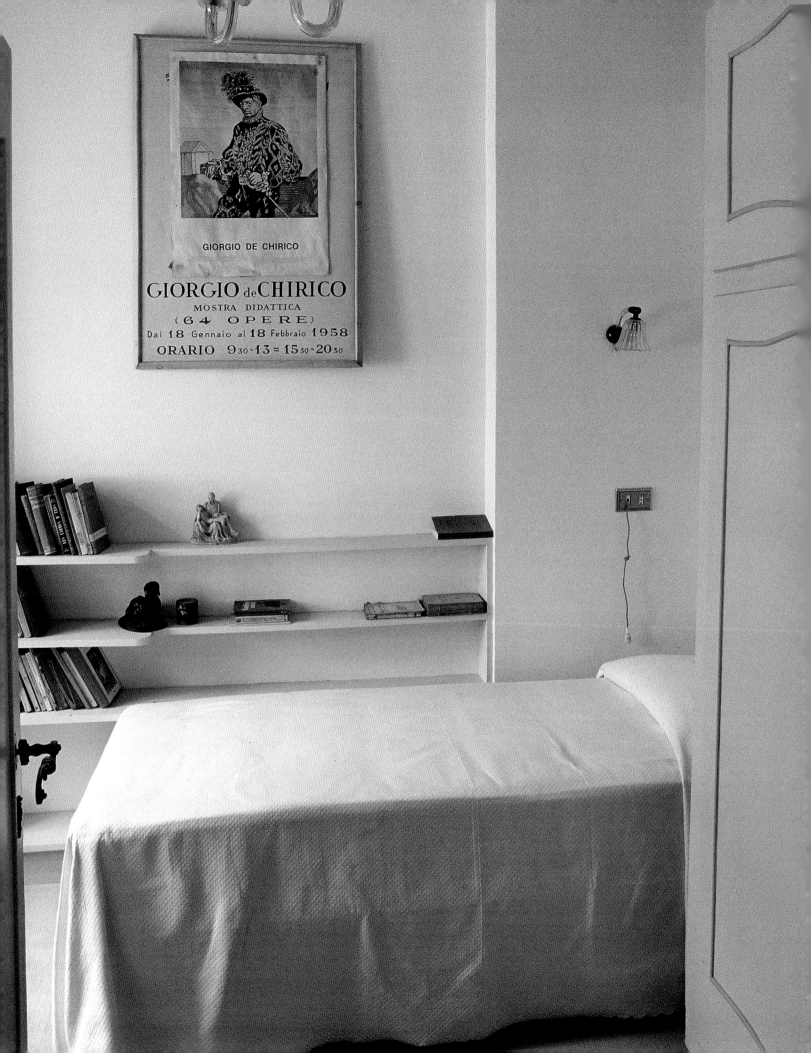

Previous spread left
The artist's Spartan bedroom is in stark contrast to the sumptuous reception rooms. The room across the passage where his wife, Isabella Far, slept was larger and more comfortable.

Previous spread right
Seated Mannequin, Giorgio de Chirico, 1926.

Above left
The passage leading to de Chirico's studio.

Above right
Paints in the studio.

Left
The artist's studio where de Chirico also kept most of his books. He was always an avid reader, and the writings of Nietzsche and Schopenhauer played a decisive role in the development of his metaphysical painting.
He was a talented writer, and his fictional work entitled *Hebdomeros*, of 1929, remains one of the greatest literary creations of the surrealist movement.

Opposite
Palette in de Chirico's studio.

"Lord, let me always improve as a painter.
Until the last day of my life, O Lord,
Let my paints help me always to progress.
Grant me, O Lord, greater intelligence and strength,
Stronger health and will,
So that I may improve my emulsions and turpentine,
So that they may always help me more..."
Giorgio de Chirico, *Morning Prayer of a True Painter*, 1942.

House Directory

ANDRÉ DERAIN
André Derain House
64 Grande rue
78240, Chambourcy
France
Tel: 013 074 7004
Email: maisonderain@free.fr
URL: http://maisonderain.free.fr

BLOOMSBURY GROUP
Charleston
Charleston Firle
Lewes East Sussex
BN8 6LL
England
Tel: 01323 811 626
Email: info@charleston.org.uk
URL: www.charleston.org.uk

FRANTIŠEK BÍLEK
Bílek Villa
Mickiewiczova 1
160 00 Prague 6
Czech Republic
Tel: 420 233 323 631
Email: pr@ghmp.cz
URL: www.citygalleryprague.cz

FREDERIC CHURCH
Olana
5720 State Route 9G
Hudson, NY 12534
USA
Tel: 518 828 0135
Email: linda.mclean@oprhp.state.ny.us
URL: www.olana.org

ALPHONSE MUCHA
Kaunick palác
Panská 7
110 00 Prague 1
Czech Republic
Tel: 420 224 216 415
Email: hlastovickova@copa.cz
URL: www.mucha.cz

RENÉ MAGRITTE
René Magritte Museum
135 rue Esseghem
1090 Brussels
Belgium
Tel: 32 2 428 26 26
Email: info@magrittemuseum.be
URL: www.magrittemuseum.be

ROSA BONHEUR
Rosa Bonheur Museum and Studio
Château de By
12 rue Rosa Bonheur
77810 Thomery
France
Tel: 33 1 64 70 51 65

GUSTAVE MOREAU
Gustave-Moreau Museum
14 rue de La Rochefoucauld
F-75009 Paris
France
Tel: 0033 1 48 74 38 50
Email: info@musee-moreau.fr
URL: www.musee-moreau.fr

WILLIAM MORRIS
Kelmscott Manor
Kelmscott
Lechlade
Glos. GL7 3HJ
England
Tel: 01367 252486
Email: admin@kelmscottmanor.org.uk
URL: www.kelmscottmanor.co.uk

GABRIELE MÜNTER
Münter House
Kottmüllerallee 6
82418 Murnau
Germany
Tel: 0 88 41 62 88 80
Email: info@muenter-stiftung.de
URL: www.muenter-stiftung.de

JAMES ENSOR
The James Ensor House
Vlaanderenstraat 27
8400 Oostende
Belgium
Tel: 32 59 80 53 35

CLAUDE MONET
Claude Monet Foundation
84 rue Claude Monet
27620 Giverny
France
Tel: 02 32 51 28 21
Email: contact@fondation-monet.com
URL: www.fondation-monet.com

ALFRED KUBIN
Kubin House
A-4783 Wernstein am Inn
Zwickledt 7
Austria
Tel: 7713 6603
Email: kubinhaus@landesmuseum.at
URL: www.alfredkubin.at

GIORGIO DE CHIRICO
Giorgio de Chirico House-Museum
Piazza di Spagna, n. 31
00187 Rome
Italy
Tel: 0039 06 679 6546
Email: fondazionedechirico@tiscali.it
URL: www.fondazionedechirico.it

Selected Bibliography

ANDRÉ DERAIN
Bell, Clive. *Since Cézanne,* Harcourt Brace, 1922.
Derain, André. *Lettres à Vlaminck: Suivies de la correspondance de guerre,* Flammarion, 1994.
Diehl, Gaston. *Derain,* Crown Publishers, 1977.

BLOOMSBURY GROUP
Bell, Quentin. *Charleston: Past & Present (Lives and Letters),* Hogarth, 1987.
Fry, Roger and Christopher Reed (eds.). *A Roger Fry Reader,* University of Chicago Press, 1996.
Garnett, Angelica. *Deceived with Kindness: A Bloomsbury Childhood,* Harcourt, 1985.
Lehmann, John. *Whispering Gallery: W.B. Yeats, Lytton Strachey, Stephen Spender, George Orwell,* West Richard, 1954.
Todd, Pamela. *Bloomsbury At Home,* Harry N. Abrams, 2000.

FRANTIŠEK BÍLEK
Bouska, Sigismund. *Sigismund Bouska Frantisku Bílkovi, korespondence 1895–1916,* Ceská expedice, 1992.

FREDERIC CHURCH
Carr, Gerald L. and Frederic Edwin Church. *Frederic Edwin Church: Catalogue Raisonné of Works of Art at Olana State Historic Site,* Cambridge University Press, 1994.
Ryan, James Anthony and Franklin Kelly. *Frederic Church's Olana: Architecture and Landscape as Art,* Black Dome Press, 2001.

ALPHONSE MUCHA
Arwas, Victor et al. *Alphonse Mucha: The Spirit of Art Nouveau,* Yale University Press, 1998.
Mucha, Jiri. *Alphonse Maria Mucha,* Rizzoli, 1989.
———. *Alphonse Mucha, The Master of Art Nouveau,* Hamlyn Publishing Group, 1967.
Runfola, Patrizia. *Le palais de la mélancolie,* Christian Bourgois, 1994.

Sayer, Derek. *The Coasts of Bohemia: A Czech History,* Princeton University Press, 2000.

RENÉ MAGRITTE
Magritte, René. *Collected Writings,* Riverrun Press, 1987.
———. *Ecrits complets (Textes Flammarion),* Flammarion, 1979.
———. *Lettres à André Bosmans: 1958–1967 (Collection Missives),* Isy Brachot, 1990.
Magritte, René et al. *Magritte/Torczyner: Letters Between Friends,* Harry N. Abrams, 1994.

ROSA BONHEUR
Ashton, Dore. *Rosa Bonheur: A Life (A Studio Book),* Studio, 1981.
De Bois-Gallais, Frédéric Lepelle. *Memoir of Mademoiselle Rosa Bonheur,* Williams, Stevens, Williams & Co., 1857.
Klumpke, Anna and Gretchen van Slyke (tr.). *Rosa Bonheur: The Artist's (Auto)biography,* University of Michigan Press, 1998.

GUSTAVE MOREAU
Lacambre, Geneviève E. and Gustave Moreau. *Gustave Moreau: Magic and Symbols,* Harry N. Abrams, Inc., 1999.
Mathieu, Pierre-Louis. *Gustave Moreau: L'Assembleur De Rêves 1826–1898,* Art Création Réalisation, 1998.

WILLIAM MORRIS
Morris, William. *William Morris by Himself: Designs and Writings,* Macdonald Orbis, 1988.
Morris, William and Clive Wilmer. *News from Nowhere and Other Writings,* Penguin Classics, 1994.
Morris, William and Norman Kelvin (eds.). *The Collected Letters of William Morris, Vol. 4 1893–1896,* Princeton University Press, 1996.
Morris, William and Philip Henderson. *Letters of William Morris to His Family and Friends,* Ams Press, 1950.

GABRIELE MÜNTER
Friedel, Helmut et al. *The Münter House in Murnau,* Prestel Publishing, 2000.
Hoberg, Annegret et al. *Wassily Kandinsky and Gabriele Münter: Letters and Reminiscences, 1902–1914,* Prestel Publishing, 2001.

JAMES ENSOR
Ensor, James. *Lettres (Archives du futur),* Archives et musée de la litérature, 1999.

CLAUDE MONET
Kapos, Martha. *The Impressionists and Their Legacy,* Barnes & Noble Books, 1995.
Monet, Claude. *Monet by Himself: Paintings, Drawings, Pastels, Letters,* Macdonald Orbis, 1989.
Russell, Vivian. *Monet's Landscapes,* American Natural Hygiene Society, 2004.

ALFRED KUBIN
Hesse, Hermann and Theodore Ziolkowski (eds.). *Soul of the Age: Selected Letters of Hermann Hesse, 1891–1962,* Farrar Straus & Giroux, 1991.
Kubin, Alfred. *La Otra Parte,* Minotauro Ediciones Avd, 2003.
Kubin, Alfred and Mike Mitchell (tr.). *The Other Side,* Dedalus, Limited, 2000.
Rhein, Phillip H. *Verbal and Visual Art of Alfred Kubin,* Ariadne Press, 1989.

GIORGIO DE CHIRICO
De Chirico, Giorgio. *Hebdemeros: With Monsieur Dudron's Adventure and Other Metaphysical Writings,* Exact Change, 1993.
———. *The Memoirs of Giorgio De Chirico,* Da Capo Press, 1994.
Taylor, Michael and Giorgio De Chirico. *Giorgio de Chirico and the Myth of Ariadne,* Philadelphia Museum of Art, 2002.

Acknowledgments

The author particularly thanks

Annie and Sergio Birga;

Petra and Valerio Cugia;

Geneviève Lacambre;

Bernard Lacombe;

Paolo Picozza.

Photo Credits